Susan Cheever

desire

Where Sex Meets Addiction

Simon & Schuster Paperbacks
New York London Toronto Sydney

Simon & Schuster Paperbacks
A Division of Simon & Schuster, Inc.
1230 Avenue of the Americas
New York, NY 10020

First Simon & Schuster trade paperback edition October 2009

SIMON & SCHUSTER PAPERBACKS and colophon are registered
trademarks of Simon & Schuster, Inc.

For information about special discounts for bulk purchases,
please contact Simon & Schuster Special Sales at
1-866-506-1949 or business@simonandschuster.com.

The Simon & Schuster Speakers Bureau can bring authors
to your live event. For more information or to book an event,
contact the Simon & Schuster Speakers Bureau at
1-866-248-3049 or visit our website at www.simonspeakers.com.

Designed by Davina Mock-Maniscalco

Manufactured in the United States of America

1   3   5   7   9   10   8   6   4   2

The Library of Congress has cataloged the hardcover edition as follows:
Cheever, Susan.
Desire: where sex meets addiction / Susan Cheever.
p.   cm.
Includes bibliographical references.
1. Sex addiction. 2. Sex. 3. Lust. I. Title.
RC560.S43C54   2008
616.85'83—dc22   20008015065
ISBN 978-1-4165-3792-2
ISBN 978-1-4165-3793-9 (pbk)
ISBN 978-1-4165-9436-9 (ebook)

acknowledgments

Like every book I have written, this book is more of a collaboration than a solo effort. Without Ron Sanders, Eliza Griswold, Jane Hitchcock, Kim Witherspoon, David Forrer, and David Rosenthal this book would never have been attempted. Without Gail Hochman, it would not have been completed. Many of the men and women who helped me would rather not be named, but they are legion. Everywhere I went, it sometimes seemed, someone had a story to tell or an idea to explain. The people whom I interviewed for the book are the heart of it, and I thank them. While I was writing, my editor Sydny Miner was invaluable both for her editing talent and her enthusiasm. All mistakes are my own, but Sydny, along with Michelle Rorke, Gypsy da Silva, and Fred Wiemer helped me to make many fewer.

My children suggested that I dedicate this book "to my children who died of embarrassment." In spite of their ambivalence about many things I have written, their intelligence, good humor, and steadfast hearts are my true inspiration.

To whom it may concern.

contents

part two: what causes it?

part three: what can we do about it?

a note to the reader

Many of the names and circumstances in this book have been changed to protect people who have told me their stories. Sex is a controversial subject even in our world of no taboos and instant information. Although as a writer I believe that nonfiction should be as close to the truth as possible, I have compromised here to protect people who have asked to remain anonymous. That this is so necessary in a book with sex and addiction as its subjects is evidence enough that we have not been able to give them the candor and compassionate openness that characterizes so much of American culture today.

If I speak with the tongues of men and of angels, but have not love, I am a noisy gong, or a clanging cymbal. And if I have prophetic powers, and understand all mysteries and all knowledge; and if I have all faith, so as to remove mountains, but have not love, I am nothing.

—St. Paul in I Corinthians

I do not like to work with patients who are in love. Perhaps it is because of envy—I, too, crave enchantment. Perhaps it is because love and psychotherapy are fundamentally incompatible. The good therapist fights darkness and seeks illumination, while romantic love is sustained by mystery and crumbles on inspection. I hate to be love's executioner.

—Stanford psychiatrist Irvin D. Yalom

The opposite of love is not hate. The opposite of love is indifference.

—Maggie Scarf

desire

part one

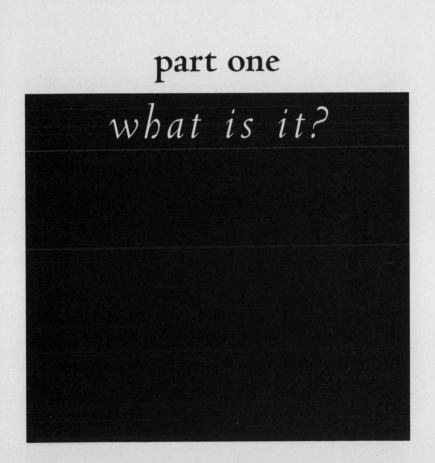

what is it?

the bride, the groom, and the dog

Standing under a black walnut tree in front of my parents' eigh-
teenth-century house on a spring afternoon, I prepared to get
married for the third time in a broad-brimmed white straw hat
and a gauzy blue and white dress. One hand held the crumpled,
preprinted wedding vows; with the other I tried to comfort my
sobbing six-year-old daughter, dressed for the occasion in a beloved
pink jumper. My heels sank into the green lawn near a shaft of June
sunlight.

Weddings make the heart soar. If second marriages are the triumph of hope over experience, as Samuel Johnson famously wrote,
third marriages may be the triumph of imagination over experience. They are even more improbable and require something closer
to delusion than simple hope. There is something delicious and
heartening about a wedding; a wedding is a chance to let our

3

dreams seem real, a frothy ceremony that is both a great party and a powerful symbol, and this is even truer when the bride and groom are experienced and knowing.

My mother had spent months planning the afternoon of the wedding, and in spite of her own ambivalence about having a daughter who was getting married for the third time, she had pulled out all the stops: there was a creamy canvas tent behind us between the walnut tree and the house, a small dance floor, platters of poached shrimp, and a gleaming, many-tiered white wedding cake decorated with garlands of flowers and a miniature marzipan bride and groom. Three hundred friends and relatives had come to Westchester from as far away as California to celebrate. The groom's family stood behind us. My two handsome younger brothers in their Brooks Brothers suits tried to calm the boisterous children from various families and the undisciplined family dogs. My mother's Labrador retriever growled to warn my corgi away from the house, while the groom's naughty basset hound explored the smells near the buffet table.

I was marrying the love of my life, a wonderful man I had been in love with for years, a man it seemed I had fallen in love with the moment he walked into a party on Potrero Hill in San Francisco where I had gone with my first husband to meet some writers. It was 1972, Richard Nixon had just been reelected by a landslide, and the Washington, D.C., police had arrested five men for what appeared to be a minor break-in at the Watergate complex. Politically, anyone left of center felt under siege. At the party, given by the journalist I. F. Stone's sister Judy, I was talking to Alvah Bessie, one of the men who had been blacklisted during the McCarthy era for refusing to answer the questions of the House Un-American Activities Committee. Bessie and Stone were our heroes.

Suddenly, there was a stir on the other side of the room near the door. I looked up and saw Warren entering the room like a king. Although we were both married to other people, and although I lived with my husband in New York and he lived with his family in San Francisco, our connection arced across all that like electricity traveling between two poles. Warren had a Victorian house with a library that he had painted deep red, a beautiful wife, two little girls, and a ditzy basset hound named Alice.

Now, seventeen years later, on our wedding day, we knew that our love had survived every obstacle—great distances, years apart, family opposition, job changes, other people's pain, our own pain, an avalanche of advice, the death of Alice, and the acquisition of Bentley, another basset. I was certain that I was marrying my great love. We had moved heaven and earth to be together. Our feelings had even endured through my marriage to someone else and subsequent divorce, Warren's divorce from the mother of his daughters, and the death of my father. Our connection was as strong as it had ever been. We made each other laugh. We continued to surprise each other. I loved him for the way his mind worked, for the generosity that had unhesitatingly invited my anxious daughter on our honeymoon, and for his passion for helping those in trouble and those with few resources. I loved him for his searching soul, which always questioned authority whether it was President Nixon's or my mother's. She had ordered us to be on time for the ceremony and bring the liquor.

Yet I was also marrying a man whose face was swollen from the effects of two days of drinking that featured a riotous bachelor party at Elaine's restaurant orchestrated by his close friends, the pornography tycoons Jim and Artie Mitchell. He was a man who bridled at the idea of signing a prenuptial agreement and had reluctantly signed a handwritten document the day before the wedding, a flamboyant character whose ubiquitous basset hound was as famously mischievous as he was. My late father had disliked him; my friends told me he was too crazy to be a good husband.

"Do you, Susan, take this man to be your lawful, wedded husband," intoned the judge, his deep voice calming the edgy crowd of guests who had already been celebrating for hours. Warren had disappeared with the best man earlier that morning, and by the time he had returned to our New York City apartment and dressed, we were an hour behind. By the time we pulled into my mother's driveway, we were two hours late. We had forgotten all about bringing the liquor. The guests had drunk everything in the house and gone out for more as the time for the wedding ceremony came and went. Every time the judge had threatened to leave, someone had offered him another drink.

At last, we were all there, standing before him as evening light began to filter through the trees. Everyone had forgotten about the dogs. One of the guests coughed behind us; my daughter continued to weep. As my husband boomed out his "I do's," he swept my white hat, ribbons flying, onto his own head. After the usual litany of how he would stand by me in sickness and health, for richer or for poorer, he managed to include a reference in the standard vows to his beloved dog.

In my family, dogs are often used to express the longings and angers we humans are too polite or too frightened to mention. When I was away at camp and miserable as a child, I got comforting letters that came not from my parents, but from the dogs, ghostwritten by my father. It was the dogs that jumped up on the cars of visitors we disliked, and stained their fancy clothes; it was the dogs that frightened away people not as attuned as we were to canine ways.

On the afternoon of the wedding, while we were distracted by the ceremony and by the impromptu blessings offered by friends who stepped to the microphone after the groom had kissed the bride, the basset hound cleverly made his move on the wedding cake. Choosing the side farthest from where we stood, he stretched his considerable length upward onto the buffet table and began to eat away at the gleaming, sugary frosting of the bottom layer, consuming enough so that the whole thing sagged dangerously to one side. By the time his theft was discovered, he had retreated to the shade of the house, his belly full, his face a mask of droopy, doggy innocence. He put his muzzle down between his big paws and looked up at us as if to say he was sorry, but it was the kind of sorry that we knew would last only until another opportunity presented itself.

My friends sometimes say that I have had bad luck with the men in my life. I don't agree. I don't think that marrying three times was my destiny any more than it was the wedding cake's destiny to be half-eaten by Bentley the basset hound, or my daughter's destiny to decide she had lost something precious at the moment we were summoned to the improvised altar under the black walnut tree.

What was going on that afternoon? Was it the happy ending to a story of two people swept away by the force of a great love? Were we in the grip of a magnificent obsession fueled by the many obstacles in its path? Were we soul mates, or were we being pulled forward by compulsions and desires that take over from reason in situations where love is concerned? Were we right to lose ourselves in the moment, or should we have paid more attention to the dog?

the broken promise

Soon after I met Warren that night in San Francisco in 1972, my husband and I went back to New York, but that made no difference. I was a journalist who got every story I could in San Francisco in order to see him, and he was an editor and writer who found every reason he could for coming to New York. Warren liked to call me late at night from the phone booth at Cookie's, a San Francisco bar that was almost his second home. I would curl up in bed in my apartment on 74th Street in Manhattan and listen. Sometimes he would nod off as I spoke, and I would hear the phone drop and bang against the walls of the booth. I would whisper my goodnights, hang up, and go back to sleep.

We had the kind of shared language siblings can have; in our precious, scarce times together it felt as if we had some connection from another life. Warren liked to say that if I were a man he would have been gay. We loved to eat good food and get pleasantly drunk, and we both loved sex. One night over stingers at the old Lion's Head, a dark pub in Greenwich Village, we agreed to have an open relationship—something of a foregone conclusion since we were both married to other people. That wasn't what we meant though; we meant that our love for each other could easily withstand the fact of our having sex with other people. Our sex was lovely, and Warren said that our love would be strengthened by what he called this separation of Church and State. It felt as though we were embarking on a great adventure, an adventure which would transcend the petty barriers and concerns that regulated the life of less fortunate human beings.

Language can hardly express a lover's confident, rapturous state of mind. "If all else perished and he remained, I should still continue to be, and if all else remained and he were annihilated, the universe would turn to a mighty stranger . . ." Catherine Earnshaw tells Nelly Dean about her love for Heathcliff in Emily Brontë's novel *Wuthering Heights*. In love, everything about the beloved seems thrilling and fascinating. "The world for him was contained within the silky rondure of her skirts," as Gustave Flaubert described the feelings of country doctor Charles Bovary about his young wife, Emma, a woman who would in turn be destroyed by her own obsession with a caddish local landowner. Yet all these characteristics: the narrowing of our world, the obsession, the experience of obstacles as an aphrodisiac, the inability to resist, are also symptoms of a kind of slavery to the substance or person that causes them.

This is a book that explores the boundaries between the kind of love on which a life together can be built, and the passionate kind of love that is an addiction and that is described by Brontë, Flaubert, and many others. When are we being drawn forward by the forces of the heart, and when are we acting in a way that will ultimately be destructive? The most familiar addictions in the world we live in are addictions to alcohol and drugs. Unlike those addictions, the addictions which use people as a substance are often hidden behind our ideas about love. Most of us want to fall in love, and we will. When we do fall in love, those who care about us will be happy. Most of us do not want to be a slave to behavior that hurts us.

"The substance I used was human beings," writes the poet Michael Ryan in his controversial 1995 memoir about his own sexual addiction, *Secret Life*. "You marshal all your intelligence and charm and power to keep the addiction alive. Getting fired by Princeton did not make me stop. Losing my wife did not make me stop. Risking my life and the lives of my sexual partners did not make me stop. Everything and everyone in your life, who you are and what you believe, falls in line around it."

How is addiction to other people different from other addictions? In our world, addiction to other people—especially addiction to sex partners—is the only addiction that is applauded and embraced. Few parents will be thrilled to hear that their child is binge drinking, using drugs, or taking out college loans and gambling them away. Most parents are delighted to find that their child has had many romantic partners. Few of us want to drink too much or become drug addicts or rack up unmanageable credit card debt, but most of us want to fall in love.

Many of us approach potential sexual partners with high hopes, and if that particular person is not "the one," we keep trying. Again and again, we may fall in love with another person or be smitten by them, and again and again we may feel that we have to back away or that we have "outgrown" them or that for whatever reason we need to move on. Nothing about this sounds alarms in our world;

everything about this is regarded as absolutely normal. The problem is that we are not addicted to just one person—the person with whom we are in love. We are addicted to the feelings of new love, of being swept away, of being adored, of being obsessed. These feelings usually last from six to eighteen months; after that it takes a new person to evoke the same feelings.

Of course, not everyone who runs through a dozen or so sexual partners in a few years is a sex addict, just as not everyone who gets so drunk that he or she can't remember what happened the night before on the drive home is an alcoholic. One big difference is that we approve of the one and disapprove of the other. Lovers get smiles; drunk drivers go to jail. "Sexual addiction is a hidden addiction; I have found more willingness to confront almost any other addiction. Sexual addiction carries a particularly large component of shame and denial with it. Paradoxically it is also one of the addictions most integrated into our society as normal," writes Anne Wilson Shaef in her study of addiction, *Escape from Intimacy*.

We are a nation of puritanical love junkies. We are passionate and we are prudish. We ban children's books that mention sex, yet our advertising often features sexualized children. Parents used to be expected to tell their children about sex in an embarrassing rite of passage; these days few parents know more about sex than their twelve-year-olds. Our befuddlement about sex is a particular part of the American DNA. Forged in the collision between the open frontier and a closed hierarchical society, this inconsistency is the basis of the American way of making love.

The United States has the highest substance abuse rate of any industrialized nation, and it is increasing fast. Studies by the Substance Abuse and Mental Health Services Administration found that between 2002 and 2005 the rate of illegal drug use among adults ages fifty to fifty-nine almost doubled. White middle-aged

Americans are the nation's fastest-growing population of abusers. National Institute on Drug Abuse statistics show that drug-related deaths have more than doubled in the last twenty years—there are more deaths, illnesses, and disability caused by substance abuse than by any other preventable health condition. (Coincidentally, a recent World Health Organization study done with Harvard Medical School found that we are also one of the most depressed nations in the industrialized world. With almost 10 percent of Americans suffering from depression or bipolar disorder, we top Lebanon, Italy, Mexico, and Japan, among others.)

The last ten years in this country have changed the way we see love and sex in two profound ways. For one thing, we have redefined privacy. The private has become public, and addictions of all kinds have been exposed. We have come to believe that public figures owe the details of their private lives to their constituencies, and that these private lives must be as much a model of probity as their public, political lives. In fact, we seem to believe that everyone—writers, actors, teachers, those who are famous for being famous—owes us the details of their private lives. The press, which once collaborated with public figures, movie stars, politicians, and other celebrities to reveal only a small part of the whole picture, now reveals everything reporters can unearth. This brave new world has caused an avalanche of sex scandals of all kinds as public figures come under a new level of scrutiny. Each year dozens of men with unimpeachable reputations—politicians, ministers, and educators—are found to have reprehensible secret lives. Some of these men are clearly sex addicts, but that is rarely mentioned in the press.

The personal lives of ordinary people have also been changed by these new standards. Reality television, television shows that dramatize personal crises, and the proliferation of memoirs have all increased our knowledge of what happens behind the bedroom, and even the bathroom, door. When I wrote a memoir about my father that was published in 1984, there were no models. I could not find one single nonfiction book in which a daughter had written candidly about her father, and only two in which a son had written about a father. When my book revealed, briefly and gently, that my father had been bisexual, the scandal of that revelation engulfed the reputation of the book. Today there are hundreds of memoirs about parents written by their children describing everything imaginable. The book you are reading at this moment, a straight look at some crooked feelings, would probably not have found a publisher twenty years ago. We have turned over the rock, and in the shadows underneath it we have often found addiction.

The second change in our world is the development of the Internet. Once the province of a few elite tech wonks, it is now open to anyone with access to a keyboard and a telephone modem or a $25 router. No more skulking around the newsstand for videos in plain wrappers: any teenage boy in a bathroom, or his mother or father on the computer at the office, can call up more provocative images and connect with more willing people than ever before. For sex addicts, one of them told me, the Internet is like crack cocaine. Part of recovery from sex addiction is having no Internet connection.

"Addiction" is the buzzword of the twenty-first century. What we call addiction ranges from the seriousness of methamphetamine addiction and the way it has changed the nature of crime, to the addictive eating disorders of upper-middle-class girls, to people who say casually they are addicted to Starbucks lattes or a certain kind of ballpoint pen, or that they are addicted to driving their new cars or sleeping on 600-thread-count sheets.

In fact, we especially seem to use the word "addiction" for

things to which we are *not* destructively addicted, like yoga classes and mystery novels and Krispy Kreme doughnuts. These are social habits, and we embrace the word "addiction" to describe them; using it erodes its power and it identifies us as someone serious, but someone who knows when to take things lightly. Many of us are addicts, but by overusing the word, we seem to get some kind of mastery over the fact, the way listening to a 911 tape over and over can make it more bearable to hear.

When it comes to our more negative addictions, we are not so flippant. These addictions may take the form of our third martini of the day or our fifth Ambien of the week or our occasional sexual infidelity when we are on the road, in another city far from home. For these actions we rarely use the word "addiction." These are our comforts, our rights and privileges, which somehow come with the difficult lives we lead. These are our ways of coping with the world. Sometimes, in the grip of a severe physical or emotional hangover, we decide not to behave in these ways. But when it comes right down to it in the sleepless night or the lonely hotel room or the uncomfortable party where everyone else is drinking, we find that we cannot resist.

Is addiction a matter of degree, or a matter of kind? A normal person can drink a few glasses of wine; in fact, normal people are currently being urged by the medical establishment to drink a few glasses of wine. A normal husband can imagine sleeping with someone else's wife. We all have desires. Addiction is defined by behavior, not by fantasy. With sexual behavior, as with alcoholism, addiction can't be measured by the amount someone drinks or their number of sexual partners. This is one of the things that makes addiction so baffling to the medical establishment and so hard to define even for those close to it. Is everyone who gets drunk an alcoholic? Certainly not. We live in a culture where more than half of college students surveyed say they regularly indulge in binge drinking. Most college students will not become alcoholics.

According to the *Columbia Encyclopedia,* addiction is "chronic or habitual use of any chemical substance to alter states of body or mind for other than medically warranted purposes. . . . Psychological dependence is the subjective feeling that the user needs the drug to maintain a feeling of well-being; physical dependence is characterized by tolerance (the need for increasingly larger doses in order to achieve the initial effect) and withdrawal symptoms when the user is abstinent."

Sex is relatively easy to define, President Bill Clinton notwithstanding. Love is even easier to define. It can be sudden—a *coup de foudre,* as the French say—or it can be gradual, but the result is the same: a connection to another person which becomes the thrilling, delicious, sought-after center of the world. Being in love can feel like falling and soaring, it can make a person hot or cold, dizzy or calm. The loved one seems infinitely desirable and the love truly transformative—when you are with him or her, you are the person you want to be, the desirable version of yourself reflected in adoring eyes.

Addiction and desire are an animal story as well as a human story. The rush of energy, the euphoria in the presence of the loved one, possessiveness and the heightened state of lovers when they are together is not exclusive to our species. Charles Darwin believed that animals loved in the way humans do and described as "love at first sight" the interaction between two ducks. Elizabeth Marshall Thomas in *The Hidden Life of Dogs* argues that dogs feel deep romantic attraction to each other. "All these data have led me to believe that animals big and little are biologically driven to prefer, pursue, and possess specific mating partners," writes anthropologist Helen Fisher in *Why We Love.* "There is a chemistry to animal attraction. And this chemistry must be the precursor of human romantic love."

With human beings, how can we distinguish between passion and addiction? One primary characteristic of addiction is *always* a broken promise, whether it's a promise made to oneself or to another person. Addicts are people who promise not to do something again and again and inevitably find that they have done it anyway. The most recognized symptom of addiction is that it causes us to do things we wish we didn't do. The addiction sweeps away all inhibitions, all good intentions, everything but need. I wanted to stop, but I couldn't, we say. This can begin in a way that seems completely harmless. Some addictions lead to ruined lives and others lead to lost sleep and some extra credit card debt, but the mechanics of the addiction are the same. Addiction is not weakness, but it is helplessness. Addiction is not a lack of willpower; it is a powerlessness over the substance in question.

It is this broken promise that causes everything about addiction in our society, from the proliferation of drug rehabs to the high divorce rate. Weddings are often ceremonies built around one of the most public and important promises many of us will make in our lifetimes. For all their solemn importance, wedding vows are often broken. "Marriages and weddings are very different things, even though the wedding industry tends to conflate them for marketing purposes," writes Rebecca Mead in her study of the American bride, *One Perfect Day*. "But the failure rate of marriages, one would think, might make selling weddings a difficult proposition. If Ford's cars or Maytag's washing machines had the same record of success as do American marriages, both companies would be out of business."

Some addictive substances are more benign than others. I sometimes stay up until two or three in the morning reading a book when I know that I have to be up at seven. I want to stop and sleep because without enough sleep my day doesn't go well, but I can't. The book holds me either with its twisted plot, which makes it impossible to put down before I have unraveled it, or with its compelling characters, who seem to be speaking to me directly from the page.

Each chapter seems to forecast the revelation or the resolution that will allow me to put in the bookmark, set the book on the floor next to my bed (the bedside table is already crowded high with books), and go to sleep. At the end of each chapter I promise myself that I will only read one more. But are these real promises? The truth is that I am enjoying myself on these late-night odysseys when the whole building is quiet and my son and the dog are fast asleep. The telephone doesn't ring, there is nothing on television except paid programming telling me how to strengthen my abdominal muscles or expand my net worth. I can read with an intensity that never happens during the day.

The seriousness of the promise that is broken may be one way to define an addiction. When two people publicly promise to stand by each other, to love and respect through good times and bad, the stakes are high. Divorce is a regrettably common form of broken promise. When I promise myself that I won't sleep with another woman's husband, I know that my peace of mind rests in the balance. When I promise myself that I will stop reading at midnight, I know that I don't really mean it.

When you break a promise you have made, whether it is a promise to yourself or to another person, you are entering the land of addiction. It may only happen once or twice. It may be an isolated incident, or it may be an unimportant promise. Still, in the same way that one cookie can lead to the whole box, one broken promise can also lead to many more. When it comes to love and the strangeness of the ways it makes us behave, and when it comes to sex with its powerful imaginative and physical pull, the first promise may feel dreadfully important. After a while though, these broken promises can come to feel natural.

Addictions come in groups. Many people whose love patterns are addictive also have eating disorders, and other addicts have even more dependency problems. A 1989 study found that more than half of cocaine users had sexual compulsion problems. After a few glasses of wine it's easier for the compulsion to overcome scruples and conscience. Overeating can diminish the pain of remorse. Addictions also often come with mental disorders in a phenomenon the psychologists call "comorbidity." According to the National Institute on Drug Abuse, 40 percent of addicts also have some underlying mental disorder.

But the effect of multiple addictions can also be to mitigate each addiction. Patrick Carnes, the man who first defined sex addiction in his 1983 book of that title, has labeled this "addiction interaction disorder." In his 2005 paper "Bargains with Chaos," written with Robert Murray and Louis Charpentier, Carnes writes that "clinicians have long noted that sex addiction was woven into an intricate web of addictions, compulsions and avoidance strategies." Studies quoted by Carnes point out that the "monodrug user" is a vanishing species in American culture.

In many cases, addictions seem to feed each other; in others they seem to starve each other. Addicts with many different substances are able to control the effects of one by using another. An alcoholic who is trying to cut back on drinking can use food, money, or sexual acting out to control the alcoholism, just as a sex addict who wants to control a string of meaningless relationships can often settle down for a while and slide into overeating, alcoholism, and money disorders.

One of the things being with Warren did for me was to hide my addictions. Warren was a larger-than-life, Rabelaisian figure; he slept with everyone he could seduce; he had no respect for functionaries, desk-hugging bean-counting types, or bill collectors. He loved to drink, beginning the day with screwdrivers and ending it with stingers. Sometimes, after finishing a particularly good restaurant meal, he would signal the waiter and order the whole thing again. Next to him I was no addict—he was the addict. In our little world I was the cautious one, the soul of moderation. When I was with him, I felt safe.

bill wilson

Seven years ago, after publishing a memoir about my own drinking life, I began reading about the life of Bill Wilson, the cofounder, with Dr. Bob Smith, of Alcholics Anonymous. I knew about Alcoholics Anonymous early on because it had saved my father's life and given us all wonderful years of family experience after he got sober. He had taken me to Alcoholics Anonymous meetings, and I loved them. As I read, I realized that there had been no definitive biography of Bill Wilson. There was one Alcoholics Anonymous–approved biography that had been written by three people and was marketed as being by Anonymous. There were many other approved books, including the book *Alcoholics Anonymous* itself, which included parts of Bill Wilson's life story. Lois Wilson, his wife, had written a memoir; his secretary Nell Wing had written a memoir; Lois's secretary had written a book about Bill. Still, there was no conventional biography, and so, although I had never written a biography, I decided to write one; it took me five years and was titled *My Name Is Bill*.

When the book was published in the winter of 2004, I went on a modest book tour. Bill Wilson was born and grew up in Vermont and I saw Vermont character and politics in many of the tenets of Alcoholics Anonymous. I drove across a snowy New England going to bookstores to read from the book. I also read in New York City, where I live, and eventually the tour took me as far south as Washington, D.C. In all these different places the question I was asked most often was this: was Bill Wilson a sex addict?

Bill Wilson was certainly an addict. Although he found a way to stop drinking, a way that became, to his amazement, a worldwide movement, he always wanted a drink and asked for whiskey on his deathbed. He was unable to stop smoking, and emphysema from smoking killed him at the age of seventy-six.

Men and women in twelve-step recovery programs have a phrase for what happens when experienced recovering addicts and alcoholics make sexual advances to newcomers—they call it "thirteenth-stepping." Alcoholics Anonymous meetings are the stage for a great deal of sexual acting out. Men and women who are feeling vulnerable and encouraged to be honest are thrown together in an intense group often once a day and almost always once or twice a week. Newcomers in A.A. are encouraged to postpone any romantic connection with the opposite sex for a year, but the suggestion is not always honored. For an alcoholic, joining A.A. can be like being released into an amazing fourth dimension, a world where honesty is normal and people help each other in order to help themselves. The very feelings the alcoholic has been chasing for so long and so unsuccessfully with a drink—calm, peace of mind, enjoyment of life—are suddenly there for the taking in a church basement or a coffee shop. It feels like a homecoming sometimes, and the people involved in it take on a special glow. It's hard not to fall in love, as it were, with the whole scene, with the friendships, with the black humor, with the people who intuitively understand, with the helpfulness of strangers; the addiction that's removed when an addict puts down a drink or a drug often resurfaces in an A.A. love affair or a series of A.A. love affairs.

Bill Wilson was famous for thirteenth-stepping. He certainly had affairs outside of his fifty-three-year marriage to Lois Wilson, and a long-term mistress, Helen Wynn, is one of the beneficiaries in his will. Wilson's father was an alcoholic whose philandering destroyed his marriage when Bill Wilson was ten years old. Many of Wilson's coworkers urged him to be more faithful and attentive to his wife. He always promised he would, but this was a promise he apparently could not keep for long.

As I interviewed Bill's colleagues, I heard story after story about Bill's inability to regulate his behavior with women. I heard that he was often accused of groping and unwelcome fondling, or fondling covered up by his status as the cofounder of Alcoholics Anonymous. I heard that, to the horror of his colleagues, he had almost been caught in a traffic stop in Brooklyn with a woman. I heard that one of them had stayed up all night with him persuading him to stay married to Lois because a divorce in 1968 would cast the shadow of scandal on the glorious progress of Alcoholics Anonymous.

When people asked me if they thought Bill Wilson was a sex addict, I gently changed the subject. I didn't want to slap a negative label onto a man I revered. My stock answer to those who were more aggressive and accused Bill Wilson of abandoning his wife and giving into sexual compulsion was that he loved his wife. They had stayed in a friendly marriage for more than half a century. This was not really the whole truth. I came to wonder if Bill Wilson was one of those people who can control his most destructive addictions only by resorting to other substances.

In the book *Alcoholics Anonymous*, published in 1941, with its cogent, well-illustrated definition of alcoholism and the stories that were really the birth of addiction studies, Bill Wilson and his co-writers discuss in detail the nature of addiction and the moments at which an addict may be ready to stop. He writes that an alcoholic must reach a "bottom," a place of despair so bitter that the alcoholic is willing to go to any lengths to stop the downward spiral created by drinking. Wilson himself was a drunk, a man who had lost all his money and his wife's money and any possibility of employment and who was headed for an institution. In going from wealth and success to poverty and broken promises, to days unaccounted for and the inability to hold even the most elementary job, Wilson noticed the progression of his own addiction from "normal" drinking with a jolly crew of friends, to coming to consciousness bleeding in a gutter with no memory of the past two days.

The early men and women of Alcoholics Anonymous had reached a point where they didn't have many options. Some were already in institutions and hospitals. In writing the book *Alcoholics Anonymous* though, Bill Wilson talked about raising the "bottom" for a new generation of alcoholics. This idea, that the symptom of an addiction can be *any* negative impact on a life—not just a catastrophic impact on a life—is at the heart of one of many controversies in addiction studies. Is an alcoholic who has lost everything the same as a man who compromises his children's graduate education by gambling? Is a woman who quietly gets drunk every night as destructive as a drunk driver? How can we quantify addiction; how can we even identify it? Does passionate sex, the fiery entanglement of two people who have fallen in love, now have to be reduced to just another symptom in a world where everything, even our most private ecstatic moments, is labeled, or can it remain a mysterious, sacred connection between two human beings?

Bill Wilson himself is an interesting test case. The questions about his private life wouldn't go away. What was even more troubling was that in some of my interviews with men who worked with Bill Wilson, they wanted to talk about his sexual behavior before they answered any other questions. Whether or not Bill Wilson was a sex addict, his desire for women threatened to jeopardize his entire life's work. Men whose lives had been saved by Alcoholics Anonymous and by Bill Wilson did everything they could to keep scandal away from the principles that were at the center of their recovery. They remembered their efforts to keep A.A. free of scandal with anger and distaste.

As part of my research for the book, I spoke to or wrote anyone I could find who had actually worked with Bill Wilson and who was still alive; Bill Wilson died almost forty years ago in January of 1971. I drove up to Calicoon, New York, to interview Tom Powers, a former advertising man. Bill Wilson and his wife, Lois, lived for the last thirty years of Bill's life in a shingle house on a hill in Bedford Hills, New York, a house they named Stepping Stones. Tom Powers had lived in nearby Chappaqua, New York, with his family and gotten sober using the twelve steps of Alcoholics Anonymous. Powers had worked closely with Bill Wilson during the 1950s as Bill was writing the long version of the twelve steps that would become the second-most-important book in the literature of the fellowship of Alcoholics Anonymous—*Twelve Steps and Twelve Traditions,* a handbook for recovery.

Powers spent many hours on the other side of Bill's desk working out what recovering people call the *Twelve and Twelve,* but he had moved out of Westchester and left Bill Wilson in 1958, going north to Calicoon to start a recovery commune of his own. Powers told me that the reason he left was Bill's sex addiction. Although it seemed clear to me, as we spoke more than forty years after the fact, that there were many feelings warring in this ninety-one-year-old man—jealousy that Bill was famous and he wasn't, anger at not being credited for his work on the twelve steps—I was amazed to hear his stories about Bill setting up two or three liaisons a day when he traveled because his need for sexual intercourse was constant.

Powers accused Bill of many things—of siphoning money to his mistress, of taking drugs—but his most persistent theme was his puritanical horror at Bill's extramarital sexual activity. As I interviewed Powers, his much younger second wife sat obediently with us as video cameras rolled to record the interview. I wanted to ask him what he thought such anger would accomplish. "Tom," I wanted to say to this old, old man, "you'll be meeting Bill soon, What will you say to him then?"

In the basement room that houses the Stepping Stones archives, I pored over every scrap of paper and image I could get my hands on looking for evidence that Bill Wilson was, or wasn't, a sex addict. There wasn't much. We don't know how Lois and Bill came to terms with his sexual nature. Many of the men I interviewed said that Bill had "stepped off the reservation," but no one had spoken to Lois about how she handled it. Author Ernest Kurtz, whose *Not God* is one of the best books about Bill Wilson and A.A., and who had complete access to A.A. records and to Lois, told me that he had been afraid to ask her about her sexual relationship with her husband. In those days, that was private information. I can imagine that. Visiting Lois, the brilliant widow of the man who started Alcoholics Anonymous, in the house where they both worked and lived could have been an intimidating experience.

As Kurtz recently wrote me in an e-mail arguing that Bill

Wilson "would not today be diagnosed as sexually addicted," it is hard to remember things in the context of forty years ago. That was a time when adultery and alcoholism were not discussed in public, or even in private, and when homosexuality was against the law. "Too many are abysmally ignorant of the context of the culture of that time," Kurtz wrote. "Can I send you back to *Life* Magazine and the Sunday supplements of the time—perhaps also to *Confidential* Magazine, not only to its 1954 story on A.A. ('No Booze but Plenty of Babes')? And then there is that marvelous source of knowledge about real life details, the fiction that appeared in 'women's magazines.'"

Still, no one seemed to have asked Lois *anything* about her attitude toward Bill's sexual behavior. I was able to locate and interview close friends of Helen Wynn, the woman who became Bill Wilson's mistress in his last years. They told me that Helen and Bill had made plans for a life together after Lois's death and that they had acquired a house in Ireland where they planned to live. They told me that Helen decided not to be around while Bill sickened and died. But I was unable to find any women who had befriended Lois or in whom she had confided.

Among Bill Wilson's biographers and men and women who have written about him or read extensively about him, there is a lot of speculation about this. Some think that Lois lost interest in sex after her two ectopic pregnancies in the 1930s when she was told that she could never bear children; some think she lost interest in sex after Bill got sober in 1935. If this is true, she may well have given him some kind of permission to stray. Whatever was true, she stayed with Bill. Publicly, and certainly a great deal of the time privately, she supported him and adored him.

It wasn't just the audiences at my readings who wanted to know if Bill Wilson was addicted to sex; some of the smartest interviewers who asked me questions about the biography on radio and television had already made up their minds that he was. Sitting in a studio in New York, I listened in surprise as Linda Wertheimer of NPR savaged Bill for his behavior in his marriage. Other interviewers accused Bill of abandoning his family. There is a lot of anger out there about men who cheat on their wives and women who cheat on their husbands; some of that anger began to come up in interviews. I was surprised, but that didn't clarify what had actually happened between Bill and Lois. Their marriage began when he was a rawboned, clinically depressed eighteen-year-old who had flunked out of school for psychological reasons and had no discernible prospects; it lasted through his successes and failures and through his drinking and sobriety. That was where I looked for answers. I told interviewers that I didn't want to judge people who had achieved a marriage of such beauty and durability.

Privately, I thought that there were many reasons why it may have been all right for Bill to sleep with other women while he was married to Lois. One of the happiest marriages I know is an open marriage—in the decades they have been married, both spouses have slept with many other people. Although my own experiments with open relationships have been mostly disastrous, I have a lot of respect for people who can stay married at all, by any means. That's what I told the interviewers.

Still, I knew there was an unhappy story hidden in the archives at Stepping Stones that I had chosen to avoid. There was no proof, but plenty of hints. There are photographs of the weekend picnics that often ended up on the Stepping Stones lawn, where sober friends and their husbands and wives gathered around Bill. In some he is leaning over pretty women while Lois occupies herself in the background. She's carrying a tray and wearing a shapeless smock while he delightedly puts an arm around a female visitor in a sundress. Then there are Bill's frequent and bitter complaints about his marriage to Lois. In a draft of an essay on himself that he wrote on yellow-lined legal pads as preparation for seeing a therapist, Bill told the story of their marriage in ugly, hurtful terms. He had been looking for a mother, he wrote. His relationship to Lois had always been that of a mother. It had never worked in any other way.

Although a great deal of bitterness and resentment had been lifted from Bill Wilson through the zealous application of his own life principles, it was clear that Lois's inability to bear children had added to the toxicity he felt at being treated like a boy—a good boy perhaps, but a boy nonetheless.

Bill was a boyish man with the quickness of youth and rugged good looks even in his early seventies. Sometimes he was a naughty boy. Even when he knew that his addiction to cigarettes was killing him, he continued to sneak a smoke. All tobacco was removed from Stepping Stones; Bill kept a concealed pack of cigarettes in his car. Everyone disapproved. This didn't seem to make any difference.

And then there was Bill's unhappiness as he lay dying, documented by nurses' records. I was working with the Stepping Stones archivist, the inspired Lynn Hoke. One morning when I went down into the archives, which are housed in the basement of a brown shingle house across from the actual Stepping Stones house, she had pulled the nurses' logs out for me. The room in the basement has an enclosed space holding the shelves and shelves of archives on movable carrels, two long tables, a computer station, and bookcases holding all kinds of books about Bill Wilson and by Bill Wilson. Photographs from the thirties hang on the stucco walls. As I stood in the corner making coffee with the little machine set out for us by Eileen Giuliani, then the director of Stepping Stones,

Lynn mentioned that she had found something interesting. She didn't say what it was.

Lynn, Eileen, and I often spent time hanging out in the basement room arguing over the circumstances of Bill and Lois's marriage. I would arrive in the morning and Eileen would come downstairs from the part of the house where she lived with her daughter, and we would start debating and remembering the events of decades past, events that sometimes seemed more vivid than the lawns and trees that we could see outside the window. When Bill and Lois Wilson had moved to Bedford Hills, it was an isolated hamlet in Westchester and the house an unheated summer cottage. Although the small town has become suburban and its ridges are now crowded with houses, the wooded plot of land around Stepping Stones still has the feel of an isolated, remote place. As we sipped coffee and let the telephone ring unanswered, we did the kind of research I love—we inhabited the lives of the people in question. Eileen identified powerfully with Lois, and she argued the case that Bill had never found the need to have sex with anyone else.

I was coming to think, although there was only indirect evidence, that Bill had done a lot of acting out sexually in general and that he had been deeply involved with Helen Wynn. There was no smoking gun, but there were letters written by Helen on her stationery from her home a few miles from Stepping Stones. These letters made it clear that Bill was living there. They referred to his health, his frame of mind, and what the two of them ate for breakfast. Lynn was a quiet participant in these girl talks, but I hoped that she agreed with me. To my mind, Bill Wilson's humanness—his inability to stop smoking, his marital problems, his need for sex—did not lessen his heroic status but made him a greater man and made his story even more extraordinary. I knew that many people didn't agree and that there were those who had worked and written about Bill who thought that any revelation showing his faults would hurt the story and the program of Alcoholics Anonymous.

That morning, I sat down to read the stack of official-looking horizontal pads, each about as big as a legal pad opened sideways. They told a sad and angry story about the weeks and days when Bill, confined to his bed at Stepping Stones, had lived out his final days breathing with the help of a machine and watched around the clock by two male nurses.

As his life wound down, Bill asked for a drink. I couldn't believe this when I read it the first time. I'm sure that the nurse could hardly believe his ears when his patient—the cofounder of Alcoholics Anonymous, a man who had been sober for more than thirty years—demanded a whiskey. Perhaps Bill was delirious, I thought. Still, there it was on the lined paper of the log in the nurses' slanted handwriting, next to the number of hours Bill had slept that night and the frequency in his use of the Bennett breathing machine that fed him oxygen. The log continued. Friends had visited and afterward Bill wept. He complained angrily about his marriage. He asked for a drink again. In the last weeks of Bill's life the nurses faithfully recorded his misery, the three times he demanded a drink and his anger when he didn't get a drink.

So when I told interviewers that Bill and Lois had been married for fifty-three years, that they had been friends at the beginning of their marriage when he was eighteen and friends at the end when he died in a Miami clinic where he had gone to try to get help for his breathing at the age of seventy-six, I was leaving out a lot. I was leaving out all the women I knew Bill had been involved with and the testimony of Tom Powers and all the stories I had been told by the men who worked with Bill over the years. Bill Wilson was a man who sometimes found life unbearable and used

a variety of ways to mitigate the pain. For years he used alcohol
with disastrous consequences. When he was able to come up with
the brilliant, inspired way of life that enabled him not to drink, he
used other substances.

For all the definitions that have been written by the hundreds
of addiction specialists and doctors, addiction is still mysterious
and baffling. In many cases it's hard to tell if someone is an addict
or just a passionate amateur. Part of the genius of Bill Wilson's program is that it leaves the definition of addiction up to the addict.
Alcoholism is a self-diagnosed disease. Anyone is an alcoholic if
they say they are—and anyone is a member of Alcoholics Anonymous if they say they are. Quite a few members of Alcholics Anonymous continue to drink. Perhaps addiction should always be
self-diagnosed. Only an addict knows when they have come to the
end, the last drink, the last trip to the casino, the last meaningless
sexual encounter. Bill's response to the baffling nature of defining
addiction was just to give it a wide berth and move on.

Before I started writing this book about sex, a friend took me
to an S.L.A.A. (Sex and Love Addicts Anonymous) meeting in
upstate New York. We parked in the lot of a church at the edge of a
perfect small-town green. Inside the parish house wide windows
looked out at the local golf course. Attractive, engaging men and
women drank coffee out of Styrofoam cups around the little table
in a room used as a nursery school classroom during the day. One
woman talked about cheating on her husband and the deep regret
she had about her own behavior. I gazed up at a child's drawing of
the sun and realized I knew exactly what she meant. All addicts
know the bite of remorse. *Agenbite of inwit*, James Joyce calls it in
Finnegan's Wake, adapting the Middle English phrase of a
fourteenth-century Benedictine monk, Michael of Northgate. Another man talked about how much he missed a woman who had

dumped him six months earlier. He was obsessed with her, and he couldn't seem to stop thinking about what closeness they had. He felt if he could just talk with her once more he might be able to change her decision. Sometimes he found himself walking past her house late at night. Outside, the lights went on in the houses on Main Street and evening fell over the greens of the golf courses. When the meeting was over, we all ambled out into the summer night and walked to our cars.

abusers vs. addicts

Doug Tieman is the president and CEO of the Caron Foundation in Wernersville, a small town in western Pennsylvania. Caron is one of the most respected rehabilitation facilities in the country. Previously, Tieman was the head of the Hazelden Foundation outside of Minneapolis, another important rehab and perhaps the most famous in the world. Hazelden's presence is so prominent that many people call the state of Minnesota "Minnesober." Tieman is a devout Lutheran, married with children, who trained to be a minister. Tall and bursting with energy, he has an answer for most questions. When he speaks, he clasps his hands behind him as if to keep himself from bouncing off the ground with conviction.

The first time I met him, he was fielding a question about why drunks should be taken to hospitals since they bring their condition on voluntarily. Drunks chose to get drunk, the question goes; why should society step in to help them out once they are drunk? Tieman calmed the questioner by noting that we live in a compassionate society. Then he pointed out that if the driver of a speeding car crashes into a tree we send all our resources to help, even though the driver has been breaking the speed law. It was an inspired answer, sidestepping the endless debate over whether or not addiction is voluntary and to what extent an addict should be held responsible for the addiction. I believe that addicts are not responsible for their addictions, but they *are* responsible for their actions, just like everyone else. But even Doug Tieman and I, united in our desires to educate people about addiction, can't really agree on what addiction is.

I have lunch with Doug Tieman at a sushi restaurant on Lexington Avenue. The restaurant cultivates a shabby look and keeps its CLOSED sign hung in the window even when it is open. After a few pleasantries we start talking about the subject. He says that 8 percent of people are alcoholics, but that 30 percent abuse alcohol. What's the difference between an addict and an abuser, I ask. Abusers, he says, can sometimes drive drunk or do other ill-advised things, but they can control their drinking if they need to. An abuser, he says is someone who can drink two drinks a day for a month, an alcoholic would not be able to do that.

I argue with Doug. If someone is driving a car with an illegal alcohol level, they are displaying the central symptom of addiction—the inability to keep a promise. Obviously, everyone decides again and again that they will never drive drunk. They promise themselves and other people that they will not drink and drive. It's against the law. It's dangerous in obvious and less obvious ways. I would say that when someone drives drunk anyway they are, by definition, out of control whether or not they can submit to other "tests" of their ability to control their drinking.

"Everyone gets one time," Doug says. He's having the

chicken teriyaki; I'm having a dragon roll. Two Japanese business-
men at the next table lean toward each other as if they are exchanging secrets. Sure, I argue, but if an abuser is someone who is
occasionally an addict, I would say they are an addict. It's like
being pregnant. You can't be a little bit pregnant. I would say that
you can't be a little bit of an addict; you can't be a beginning
addict. You are or you are not. Doug Tieman and I spoke to each
other that day in October 2006 as two responsible people, people
who had somehow come to terms with ourselves and had turned
to helping others. But addiction is cunning and powerful. In
March of 2008, Doug Tieman was arrested for drunk driving
in Palm Beach, Florida, as he made his way home at 3 A.M.

With sex and sexual obsession, the line between an addict and
an abuser is even fuzzier than it is with alcohol. If you can occasionally drive drunk and still not be an alcoholic, certainly you can occasionally cheat on your husband or wife and still not be a sex addict.
Of course, there are sex addicts who have to sleep with two or three
people a day almost every day. There are men and women who don't
feel alive unless they are involved in seduction and sexual gratification, just as there are alcoholics who drink vodka all day every day.
These clear-cut cases are rare though, and it's the less black and
white variety of addiction that has the potential to confuse us.

Drinkers who "control" the drinking enough so that others
don't notice and so that there are no jail stays or automobile accidents may still be drinking enough to erode the inner fabric of their
lives; sex addicts who only "occasionally" sleep with someone they
have decided not to sleep with can look all right from the outside
but be compromising their ability to connect with another human
being in any satisfying, lasting way. Addiction is a disease of the
soul. The body may also show scars, but it's the emotional and spiritual life of the addict that shows the real symptoms.

If the first symptom of addiction is a broken promise, the second is often a feeling of remorse. An addict, after giving into the addiction and doing what he or she has definitely decided not to do, typically feels awful. Suddenly wrapped in the hotel sheets, the sex addict feels nauseous. The smells of sex that were intoxicating just a few minutes before seem revolting. In drinking, remorse is often accompanied by a hangover. In *How We Die*, Sherwin Nuland calls addiction "chronic habitual suicide."

A third symptom of addiction is the way in which longing for the substance seems to be fed by deprivation and also by satisfaction. With a normal hunger or a normal yearning—a hunger for a good meal or a hunger for a good night's sleep—there is the possibility of satiation. After eating we feel satisfied and full. Upon awakening we feel rested. These desires for sleep, food, water, and physical comfort are drives rather than addictions. Addiction exists outside these natural rhythms. An addict is desperate when the substance is scarce, but almost equally desperate when the substance is available. There is no cause and effect. Whatever "it" is, the addict always wants it and can never have enough of it. The more they have, the more they want. This is the quality that narrows the addict's life down to the acquisition of a reliable supply, whether that is a group of willing men or women for the sex addict or a pantry filled with vodka for the alcoholic.

"Addiction makes love impossible," writes bell hooks in *All About Love*. "Most addicts are primarily concerned with acquiring and using their drug, whether it be alcohol, cocaine, heroin, sex or shopping. Hence, addiction is both a consequence of widespread lovelessness and a cause."

According to Erich Fromm in his classic *Art of Loving*, emphasis on materialism and conformity in our capitalist society has rendered love obsolete and impossible. "No objective observer of our

Western life can doubt that love . . . is a relatively rare phenomenon and that its place is taken by a number of forms of pseudo-love which are in reality so many forms of the disintegration of love. . . . Automatons cannot love; they can exchange their 'personality packages' and hope for a fair bargain."

A few weeks after I had lunch with Doug Tieman, I flew to Washington, D.C., for a Caron Foundation press conference with Patrick Kennedy, a congressman who has been sober since being stopped by the D.C. police after a car accident. The purpose of the press conference, held in the shadow of the Capitol on the terrace of the Cannon House Office Building, was to get attention for a parity bill. Insurance companies do not want to treat addiction and mental illness in the same way that they treat other diseases; they do not want to pay for treatment. This bill would force them to deal with addiction as if it were any other disease. It would make treatment in the form of rehabilitation, counseling, and other proven methods for helping addicts available to many people who had not been able to afford help.

We stood there in the cool morning as Doug Tieman made his eloquent pitch to the cameras. He was followed by Kennedy and Kennedy's cousin Christopher Lawford, a recovery activist whose memoir *Symptoms of Withdrawal* is an inspired portrait of addiction of all kinds.

The last speaker was a doctor who brought up a subject that is the focus of many studies of addiction—the subject of medication for addiction based on chemical changes in the brain tracked through sophisticated imagery. Since the patterns of addiction can now be tracked as they occur in the human brain, the prospect of drugs to interrupt and change those patterns has become a holy grail for some people in the medical community.

Sexual performance and its connection to brain chemistry has also recently been changed by the advent of new drugs—Viagra, Levitra, Cialis— which override the body's natural functions, jump-start the vascular system, and allow erections on demand. Viagra may soon be obsolete, replaced by a drug called PT-141 currently in its second round of testing for FDA approval. PT-141 is not a vascular drug like Viagra; it does not restrict its effect to a few blood vessels. It is a true aphrodisiac, altering the brain chemistry of those who take it and giving them a tremendous sensual-desire high. For years love potions have been the stuff of story, from Shakespeare's zany *Midsummer Night's Dream* to Jerry Leiber and Mike Stoller's "Love Potion Number Nine." Their lyric about a potion which smells like turpentine and looks like Indian ink and has an immediate effect—*I didn't know if it was day or night, I started kissing everything in sight*—is as good a description of a dopamine rush as any.

Time with Warren always felt like this kind of ecstasy as we continued to commute between New York and California to see each other. There were many other obstacles. After a year or so, my first husband guessed that I had fallen in love with Warren; I was tired of lying about it. We separated, and so I was free to spend more and more time in San Francisco, although by that time I had a good job in New York at *Newsweek* and Warren had started up a new magazine in San Francisco, *City,* financed by Francis Ford Coppola. My best girlfriend in San Francisco was Susan Berman, a witty, energetic reporter for the *San Francisco Examiner* who had been sharp enough to guess that I wasn't spending so much time in San Francisco because of work. We were both daughters of famous men—Susan's father was reputed mobster Davie Berman, an associate of Meyer Lansky. I introduced her to Warren and she began to write for his magazine. Sometimes the three of us had dinner together; sometimes, if she was away, she loaned us her apartment.

She became my confidante and a kind of vivacious third party in my relationship to Warren. She was attractive, crackling with ideas, and had inherited some money, but she couldn't seem to find a boyfriend. She wrote a cover story for Warren at *City* about this titled "Why San Francisco Girls Can't Get Laid."

Warren was always hard to reach: sometimes he was with his family; sometimes he was on deadline. I had told him I was sleeping with a *Newsweek* colleague; he told me that Susan wanted to sleep with him. I didn't protest (how could I?), but when I realized that Warren *was* sleeping with Susan Berman, I found—to my surprise—that I was furious. Furious at my friend who had betrayed me, furious at my lover who had also betrayed me, and most of all furious at myself for not having been able to admit how these betrayals would feel. She wrote a smug little story in *City* about sleeping with the editor, and I claimed my anger was about the publicity. Warren stopped sleeping with Susan Berman, and I stopped speaking to her.

Warren and I made up; he did a special issue of the magazine that bought him some time to spend in New York. Was I still angry? A few months after the Susan Berman debacle, my father introduced me to a handsome, married writer with whom I began an affair. I told Warren about it; I said he owed me one. Neither of us knew that this time our relationship was heading for a cliff.

Later, Susan Berman wrote a novel and a memoir about growing up in Las Vegas, and she moved to Los Angeles. I ran into her once on Madison Avenue in New York City; I smiled wanly and kept on walking. On Christmas Eve of 2000 she was murdered, shot to death by someone who was even angrier than I was about something she had said or done.

the brain

Scientists are now able to photograph the brains of drug addicts and alcoholics to show how the substance affects the user. Their photographs of the brains of people in love are almost identical to photographs of the brains of people on drugs. In other words, falling in love as we know it is an addictive experience. "Directly or indirectly, virtually all 'drugs of abuse' affect a single pathway in the brain, the mesolimbic reward system, activated by dopamine," writes anthropologist Helen Fisher in *Why We Love: The Nature and Chemistry of Romantic Love.* "Romantic love stimulates parts of the same pathway with the same chemical. In fact, when neuroscientists Andreas Bartels and Semir Zeki compared the brain scans of their love-stricken subjects with those men and women who had injected cocaine or opioids, they found that many of the same brain regions became active."

In a now-famous experiment in which people who were "madly in love" were shown photographs of their loved ones, Fisher and her colleagues Arthur Aron and Lucy Brown demonstrated that the parts of their brains linked to pleasure—the ventral tegmental area and the caudeate nucleus—lit up when their brain registered the beloved images. The caudeate nucleus contains many receptors for dopamine—a chemical that acts like a personal love drug. Dopamine combines with other chemicals to create what some scientists call a "pleasure pathway" and others a "hedonistic highway" in the chemistry of the brain. It's not just dopamine that lovers and addicts are craving. "One of the most important chemicals to be released when lovers meet is phenylethylamine, an amphetamine-like cocktail that raises mood and energy levels," writes Dr. Frank Tallis in his book *Love Sick: Love as a Mental Illness*.

As they are released into the brain, these love drugs create intense energy, focused attention, and motivation to win rewards. This is why, as Lauren Slater has written, "when you are newly in love you can stay up all night, watch the sun rise, run a race, ski fast down a slope ordinarily too steep for your skill. Love makes you bold, makes you bright, makes you run real risks, which you sometimes survive and sometimes don't."

Fisher, who has been called the "doyenne of desire," expands on the parallels between addiction to drugs and addiction to love. "Moreover, the bewitched lover shows the three classic symptoms of addiction: tolerance, withdrawal, and relapse. At first the lover is content to see the beloved now and then. But as the addiction escalates they need more and more of their drug."

The similarities don't stop there but continue throughout the life of a relationship or an addiction. Withdrawal from a loved one creates the same kind of agony the heroin user goes through with the "bone-crushers" of withdrawal or the dreadful withdrawal of an alcoholic's seizures, shakes, and delirium tremens. "If the beloved breaks off the relationship, the lover shows all the common signs of drug withdrawal, including going to greater and greater lengths to procure the 'drug' or to see the beloved person," Fisher explains.

In one essay on romantic rejection Fisher begins with a poem recited by an anonymous Kwakiutl Indian to a missionary in 1896:

Fires run through my body—the pain of loving you. Pain runs through my body with the fires of my love for you. Sickness wanders my body with my love for you. I remember what you said to me. I am thinking of your love for me. I am torn by your love for me. Pain and more pain. Where are you going with my love? I'm told you will go from here. I'm told you will leave me here. My body is numb with grief. Remember what I've said my love. Goodbye my love, goodbye.

Fisher points out that there are even further parallels. Lovers tend to relapse just as addicts tend to relapse. A place where he or she has been especially happy with the beloved, a significant song, an encounter with a mutual friend, the smell of a particular perfume can trigger the craving and the pain of withdrawal.

If, as Fisher writes and documents, falling in love has a brain chemistry almost identical to the brain chemistry of one who takes hard drugs or other addictive substances, then sex and love addiction is a double-barreled problem. What Cupid shoots is more like a shotgun than an arrow. The normal pleasure pathways in the brain are doubly lit up both by the dopamine and other chemicals in response to another person and by the process of addiction. This is why, often, sex addiction seems to be the most powerful addiction and the one behind many cases of alcoholism, drug abuse, and other addictions.

Our thirst for love is our very first emotional experience. Our connection with other people and our longing for them begins as soon as we have feelings, even the inchoate feelings of the infant. Babies long for their parents and coo with pleasure when they are held in the familiar arms. The yearning and the brief requital followed by more intense yearning that characterizes an addiction is an experience we have all had almost since we were born—an experience from the time before we can remember.

What makes love and sex addiction even harder to understand and treat is that sex is not an illegal substance in our culture. When you tell your friends you are addicted to cocaine, they will be concerned; they will look for help. When you tell your friends that you are buying a new car, they will wrinkle their brows and ask if you are sure you can afford it; they will advise you about makes and models and payment plans. But when you tell them you are in love, even that you are in love with a man you shouldn't be in love with, they will smile knowingly and often give you their blessing.

For all these reasons it is difficult to overestimate the power of emotional addiction to another person—whether brief, as it is in casual sexual encounters, or lengthy, as it can be in drawn-out love affairs. Sex addiction is the superpower of addictions. It has a history as old as Ovid, who in *The Art of Love* advises the afflicted to consume white onions from Megara, honey, pine nuts, and radishes. It is as carefully considered as the experiments of psychiatrist Michael Liebowitz, who suggested that the chemistry of love might be divided into different phases of parallel drugs: amphetamines and stimulants, narcotics and sedatives, and chemicals that enhance appreciation and spiritual feelings like mescaline and LSD.

By the time I visit Helen Fisher in her pleasant apartment off Fifth Avenue in Manhattan, I feel as if I already know her from watching her on my computer screen. I have seen a video of her giving a speech in California, and read her books as well as a dozen articles. I have compared official photographs of her looking a lot like Holly Hunter to more casual photographs that show a distinguished, pretty sixty-something woman sitting on the ground in Africa with friends and anthropological subjects. I like Helen Fisher right away. She lives in an apartment that's all hers—there are no dogs or cats or traces of children or a husband or family photographs. Instead there are books, dark gleaming furniture, and a large red and blue oriental rug.

As we chat about definitions, Fisher separates addiction from love in a way I haven't heard: the definition has three parts. The first stage of desire is a drive, a simple craving for gratification. "You can feel this for a number of partners, it's like hunger or thirst," she explains. This drive, or pure sex addiction, has nothing to do with another person. The obsession is with the orgasm, not the individual. When the brain is photographed in this stage of desire, it shows that drive—if we call this stage drive—is located in the amygdala and the hypothalamus. This drive is both overwhelming and easily satisfied.

The second stage of desire is what Fisher calls romantic love. This kind of love is focused on just one person, Fisher explains, and it is associated with a generalized euphoria. Brain imagery shows that this is the desire that lights up the dopamine pathways and hijacks the brain's reward system. This is hedonistic, addictive desire, desire that trips over into obsession, the addictive trance and damaging acting-out—the subject of literature and of this book.

Fisher describes a third state of desire that she calls attachment. If drive and romantic desires have evolved in order to allow men and women to propagate the race, attachment has evolved in order to enable us to "tolerate another person long enough to raise a child," Fisher says with a laugh.

As an anthropologist, Fisher sees the world in terms of

humans' adaptive behavior: women search for new mates after a year or two in order to expand their genetic possibilities and add to their financial resources; the three stages of desire are escalating connections which enable men and women to bear and care for children. The brain, built when there was a stable community for raising children, is now causing trouble as we become isolated nomads. According to Fisher, our growing addiction problem is really an adaptation problem. Our brains were formed in order to survive in the kind of world that no longer exists.

Helen Fisher is a philosopher, an anthropologist, a writer who spends her days reading everything from psychological studies to literary classics as well as setting up and conducting psychological experiments. Recently, she has been recruited by an Internet dating service to help with their questionnaires, and she has developed a series of personality profiles to help narrow the field of prospects for each customer.

Dr. Nora Volkow approaches addiction from yet another direction—as a medical doctor studying only the results of addiction on brain chemistry—but in many ways she has come to the same conclusions. A pale, intense woman with a slight accent, she often points out that we are fascinated when people actually continue a behavior they desperately want to stop. The great-granddaughter of Leon Trotsky, Volkow grew up in Mexico in the house where the revolutionary was killed in 1940. As a young doctor, she became interested in addiction, in the ways people act against their own wishes. She has written hundreds of papers on addiction and is currently the director of the National Institute of Drug Abuse (NIDA), which is part of the National Institutes of Health.

Dr. Volkow explains that the body has a natural reward system, a system of dopamine pathways set up to help us survive. These rewards kick in when we find food or find a mate or realize any of the other behaviors that are healthy for our species. Drugs also activate the dopamine system, she says.

But Volkow's research has unearthed a new dimension of this problem. Drugs are more efficient than the normal behavior that floods the brain with pleasure. Once someone experiences this heightened, abnormal level of pleasure, their brain begins to crave it instead of wanting the normal levels of pleasure. In love the brain buzzes with just enough pleasure to enable a man and a woman to couple and have children. In addiction the pleasure is more intense than it needs to be. The drugs or the addictive behavior provide the brain with a more efficient delivery system and the addict experiences a dopamine spike—an unnatural level of pleasure which, when it subsides, leaves pleasure levels lower than normal.

Soon the drug, or the behavior, is necessary for the addict to feel normal. At that point the addict's brain also needs more and more of the drug to feel the pleasure. Normal pleasure sources have no effect. The brain exists in what feels like a state of deprivation, and using the drug comes to feel necessary for survival.

In the case of sex and love the pattern is slightly different. The normal brain is set up to have a dopamine rush during sex because sex is one of those behaviors that enable us to survive. But then, in some people, at some times, something goes wrong. Some sexual experiences appear to have the same effect as a dopamine spike. People for whom this happens are at risk for an intense addiction to other people. Do some people enjoy sex more than others? Does sex have some emotional or physical charge for some that it lacks for others? Why are some people able to go through life sleeping with one or two partners, while others seem insatiable when it comes to sexual partners? "We all think we can control our actions," Volkow says, "but why does one person have such intense cravings that they experience a loss of control, while another person can overpower these desires?"

On camera in an HBO special on addiction, Volkow interviews a normal-looking man who is addicted to methamphetamine. She shows him the holes in his brain where the addiction has stripped his dopamine receptors. He is forty-three but he has the brain of an eighty-year-old. What's the difference between addictions? Is the brain of a sex addict, a man or woman who is unable to stay married because of sexual need, or a man or woman who is unable to abstain from having sex with students, the brain of an older person too? What about the brain of someone dependent on nicotine, or someone with an eating disorder who is consistently thirty pounds overweight? When it comes to brain chemistry, where does addiction begin?

trance and obsession

"It's as if an electronic magnet in my solar plexus was switched on. At its most intense I'd go into a kind of trance, dissociated, beamed in from Mars, my mouth dry and my heart pounding, my usual waking consciousness hovering somewhere outside my body while I was taken in by the pull," writes Michael Ryan. One of the most mysterious and creepy symptoms of addiction is this kind of trance. An addict will decide not to do something, whether it's not to use a credit card or not to drink more than one glass of wine or not to go home with the drug dealer. The decision is usually carefully considered and based on previous painful experience. The decision is final. The addict is sure. Later, when the addict can't understand how she could have done what she had promised not to do, it seems in memory to have been a trance.

In 1978, *City* magazine folded, and *Newsweek* was ready to transfer me to San Francisco. The obstacles to Warren's and my great love were removed, but I had become deeply involved with the handsome writer who had left his wife and moved in with me. In moments of precious sanity, I told myself and my friends that, although I would always love Warren, I had realized that I could not build a life with him. My passion for the writer might not be the blazing, excruciatingly painful connection I had with Warren, but he was a wonderful, responsible, witty, and intelligent man, and I loved him too, in a different way. Warren protested, of course. He came to New York to try to change my mind; it was too late. I was sick of his lateness and his wildness and sick of all that pain. Visiting him in his room at the raffish Chelsea Hotel, I noticed that there was a crumpled cigarette package under the bed. Warren didn't smoke.

With the writer's encouragement, I left my job at *Newsweek* and wrote a novel, *Looking for Work*, which was published in 1980. I married the writer; we had a wonderful daughter. I didn't speak to Warren for almost four years. I told myself that I felt lucky to have escaped. Then one morning, when my husband and I happened to be in San Francisco for a week, I called Warren. He met me in the lobby of the hotel, and in some ways it was as if we had never been apart. We stood in the hotel bar and talked until it was time for me to meet my husband for dinner. Warren said things about writing that surprised me, and as always, his liberal use of profanity was refreshing, like a blast of honesty and anger blowing through my carefully constructed married-lady world.

Still, I was wary. I was a happily married woman. I told myself we would just be very good friends, friends who had shared the amazing experience of being truly in love with each other, friends whose concern for each other had transcended our once-passionate sexual connection.

The next spring Warren was in New York for a visit; he was writing a column for the *San Francisco Examiner.* His boss, Will Hearst, had become a good friend and was a generous employer. We arranged to have lunch, and I said I'd pick him up at the Essex House, the hotel where he was staying on Central Park South. I would have lunch with him, but I would not sleep with him. I had many good reasons not to sleep with him; I was married and I did not want to jeopardize my marriage and my beloved family. I left our apartment in a glow of certainty.

I took a cab down to the Essex House and went up to the desk. Warren had said he would meet me in the lobby. Of course, he wasn't there. The man behind the desk gave me the room number and directed me to a house phone. I stood in the alcove and picked up the phone, and that's the last thing I remember. I seemed to go into some kind of brownout. I can hardly reconstruct what happened. Warren told me to come up to his room and I did. It was a big sunny room strewn with intriguing magazines, newspapers, and books. I made myself comfortable while he got dressed to go out. Then, somehow we were on the bed. Before I was back in command of my own actions, we were, indeed, having lunch under very different circumstances than what I had imagined. How did that happen?

I experienced the same thing with eating and drinking. When an addict says that she didn't mean to do it, when the addict says that something else took over, she isn't kidding. It sounds like an excuse, but it's a dreadful fact of the way addiction works. Giving in to the substance is as involuntary as breathing; you can hold your breath for a while, but in the end you give in.

Addicts throughout history have struggled to describe this out-of-body feeling that takes over when they abuse their substance after making many promises that they won't. In Alcoholics Anonymous, newcomers who are still at risk for this trance state are said to be *mocus*—a word created by combining "mind" and "out of focus." In Debtors Anonymous this fugue state is called "terminal vagueness" and it's a good description.

"Every Thursday at noon I have sex with Rick in room #213 of the Rainbow Motel. Today, even though I promised my therapist I wouldn't come here again, I pull into the lot and park beside Rick's black Ford Bronco. I cut the engine and listen to stillness, to nothing, to heat," writes Sue William Silverman in her sex addiction memoir, *Love Sick*. She and Rick are both married, but neither can resist the lure of their meetings. "For months, like a mantra, my therapist has told me, 'these men are killing you.' I don't know if he means emotionally, spiritually or physically. I don't ask," Silverman writes. "He explains that I confuse sex with love, compulsively repeating this destructive pattern with one man after another. I do this because as a girl I learned that sex is love from my father, the first dangerous man who sexually misloved me.

"'I thought the intensity with Rick must be love,' I say.

"'The intensity is an addict's high,' my therapist says. 'Not love.'"

Those who are hurt by the addiction are often scornful of the way an addict describes being taken over by the addiction, and who can blame them? "I didn't know what I was doing," doesn't sound like much of an excuse. But this almost otherworldly suspension of the will and the reason is actually a symptom of addiction. An addict is someone who comes to, who regains normal consciousness—either in the morning or at another time of day—and asks what happened, not to evade responsibility but because the things that happened really seem to have happened to someone else. In a way, this is one of the principal problems of getting addiction the attention it needs. Normal people find it hard to believe in the addictive trance.

"I didn't know what I was doing" isn't much comfort to a woman whose husband has been unfaithful or a parent whose child has been killed by a drunk driver, or even a headmaster who discovers a student in the bathroom with a six-pack of beer. Not only does the truthful description of the addictive experience—and it isn't easy for addicts to tell the truth—sound phony, but it also sounds as if the addict is trying to avoid responsibility.

It is hard for an addict to tell the truth, and the addict is rarely rewarded for the attempt. Early on, addicts learn to lie, and there is something about the protection of lies, the slippery, easily acceptable surface of saying what people want to hear, that is extremely seductive. Addicts often become adept at lying and reluctant to tell the truth even when there is no harm in the truth. The addict leads a secret life. This is both one of the thrills and one of the symptoms of addiction. When addicts find each other, and they seem to have some secret way of knowing who they are, they often bond over a shared lie. After all, there is something exciting about learning to lie, something exciting about knowing that even those closest to you don't really know you. Our world is filled with lies; addicts find a way to use those lies to separate themselves from other people and to protect their addictions.

One of the most famous symptoms of addiction is obsession. *Romeo and Juliet* is a story of obsession as is *Heloise and Abelard, Anna Karenina,* and many other classic novels and poems. Obsession is like the flu of the mind. Once excited, it takes over people who are obsessed. Their entire being is focused on the object of the obsession. In the morning they wake up, and when they turn over, it's as if a light turns on in the soul—the obsession is there. Obsessions usually have little to do with the actual people who inspire them, but knowing this is no help at all to the person who is doing the obsessing. In fact, nothing the mind knows has much effect on what the brain does when it latches onto an object of obsession.

Sexual obsession is one of the great sources of energy in human history; it has led men and women to declare wars and write books and travel around the world. It is also the subject of a lot of great literature, from the Homeric masterpiece *The Iliad*—obsession started the Trojan War when Paris became obsessed with Helen—to Vladimir Nabokov's *Lolita,* which is about the obsession of a middle-aged man with his stepdaughter.

Anna Karenina is about the obsession of a young married woman with a man who, although perfectly good-hearted and obsessed with her as well, drives her to her death. "He felt that all his hitherto dissipated and dispersed forces were gathered and directed with terrible energy towards one blissful goal. And he was happy in that," Leo Tolstoy writes of Count Vronsky after he has declared himself to Anna on the platform of the Moscow–St. Petersburg train. "He knew only that he had told her the truth, that he was going where she was, that the whole happiness of life, the sole meaning of life, he now found in seeing and hearing her."

Madame Bovary, Jane Eyre, and *Wuthering Heights* are about obsession. Much of great poetry, from the sonnets of Shakespeare to William Butler Yeats to Emily Dickinson, is about obsession. "To lose thee were to lose myself," Adam tells Eve in Milton's *Paradise Lost.*

Obsession is so extreme and so hard to imagine with the rational mind that it has a science-fiction–like quality to it—it's almost as if the obsessed one has been taken over by a replica, a pod, a facsimile of the rational person. When one is in the grip of an obsession, everything else—children, regular meals, sleep, work—is swept away. The entire being is one yearning, frothing bath of desire. It's the dirty trick of obsession that getting its way—spending time with the object of desire, having sex with the object of desire—doesn't lessen the obsession, but increases it. Although an addict, while obsessed, truly believes that being with the object of the obsession will cure the obsession, the opposite is true. When an alcoholic promises that all he needs is one last bender to achieve satisfaction, he's chasing a chimera.

Once obsession takes over, few things can loosen its grip. Yet it can pass as rapidly as it descends, leaving only traces in the memory. For a while when I was in my fifties, I was entirely obsessed with a man named Bob. The obsession lasted a year or more. I thought about him, talked about him, remembered our times together, and imagined new times together almost every waking minute. Once the obsession lifted—and this was after a painful and lengthy process of breaking up—I was amazed at what I had gone through. I didn't share much with him. He disapproved of my friends, and they returned the favor. He was jealous of my children and dismissive of my work. Being with him didn't make my life better or help the things I really cared about. What was I thinking?

Normal people have some experience with obsession. For an addict it is an almost constant state of mind—a state of mind that seems real, compelling, and which makes it important to do everything possible to grant the obsession's requests.

"The addict uses—or abuses, rather—one of the most exciting moments in human experience—sex," writes Patrick Carnes in *Out of the Shadows*, first published in 1983 under the title *The Sexual Addiction*. "Sexual arousal becomes intensified. The addict's mood is altered as he enters the obsessive trance. The metabolic responses are like a rush through the body as androgens speed up the body's functioning. The heart pounds. . . ." Carnes is the godfather of sex addiction. He works at the Pine Grove center in Mississippi, but he spends most of his time lecturing around the country. He has irritated many people by saying that Bill Wilson was a sex addict; he has helped many people. Coincidentally, we both studied at Brown University in the 1960s; I was an undergraduate, and he was getting a masters degree in European history and working toward a doctorate. When he flunked his doctoral exams and the university refused to let him retake them, he tells me, "I thought it was God's punishment for my sexual acting out." I could hardly believe my ears. At Brown, I was a sexual beginner; it seemed to me that there was very little sex going on. My parents had spent a great deal of time telling me that I was unattractive and would never find a husband. Later in life I surrounded myself with lovers, many of whom I brought home to my parents, so many that the guestroom in their house was called "the boyfriend room." Perhaps proving them wrong was one of my motivations; if so, I didn't realize that at the time. But as a college freshman I still accepted their verdict.

Obsession is destructive, but we love it. In spite of a great deal of evidence to the contrary, in spite of horrifying domestic violence figures, for instance, we often insist on seeing it in a benevolent light. There is a perfume named Obsession. We say we are obsessed with a man or woman we have just met and our friends smile knowingly. We do the same thing with the word "obsession" that we do with the word "addiction"—we trivialize it through overuse.

We are obsessed with a dress we want to buy, we will say, or we are obsessed with getting an A, or we are obsessed with our hair. We don't use the word so freely when we are referring to its dark side. Not only is obsession the goad that drives men and sometimes women to hurt and kill the people they say they love—and sometimes their children as well—but in taking up the whole mind it diminishes the person it possesses. Instead of thinking about writing an essay or solving a math problem or how to sell more insurance, the victim of the obsession can only think about one thing—the object of the obsession.

"The obsessor is both the hurricane and the house it destroys," explains the writer Jane Stanton Hitchcock. "A 'love' obsession—an oxymoron if there ever was one—is the most frequent type of obsession. The obsessor concocts a scenario, then enacts it with almost total disregard to reality. It usually runs something like this: 'I am so in love with this person that even though he/she treats me badly, I have to put up with him/her because there's no one else for me in the world and never will be.' Wrong."

Yet obsession serves a purpose. By blotting out all other thoughts, it eliminates fear. We are afraid of dying, we are afraid of illness and indigence, we are afraid our children will come to harm, we are afraid to lose things we already have, things that we have earned. We are afraid that in the future we won't get what we need. We scare ourselves with our own thoughts of despair—maybe we should step in front of a bus—and rage—if we had had a gun there are many times when we might have used it. This is what it means to be human, but it's scary.

A temporary, high-cost cure for these thoughts and feelings that worry us is obsession. If we are obsessed, we don't think about anything else. We don't have creative urges. We don't plan our next vacation. Instead we are living fantasies of what might happen with the object of our obsession and combing the past for clues about the object of our obsession and treasuring past moments with the object of our obsession. We are useless, but we are protected by the invisible wall of obsession from the terror that wakes us up at three in the morning and won't let us go back to sleep. In this way obsession, a symptom of addiction, actually functions as an addiction itself. It blocks out the world.

For me, obsession started with men. It happened in my sophomore year at college when a student I had a crush on from a distance began calling me. All my friends also had crushes on this man, but it was me that he called. Obsession loves company. I would see him across the leafy campus during the day—Brown has a setting of beautiful nineteenth-century buildings laid out on a gentle hill above the city of Providence, Rhode Island. I was living in a grey shingle house on one of the side streets near the campus with a dozen other sophomore girls. The house had one phone and a message book next to the phone. When the phone rang, whoever was closest to it answered, and yelled out the name of the girl being called at the top of her lungs. If there was no response, she took a message and wrote it in the book.

I lived in a tiny room at the back of the house, looking out onto the lawns and the backs of other wooden houses on the hill. One evening the phone rang and it was him calling for me. We went for a walk in the spring twilight, in air which seemed charged with our feelings for each other. The next night he called again; we held hands. Some nights he didn't call, and these nights were spent wondering where he was and what he was doing. My own life faded to black and white while his life—as I imagined it—was vivid and constant.

This went on for a few weeks. Around noontime I began to worry about whether or not he would call that night. At twilight the tension became almost unbearable. I would sit frozen in my room waiting for the distant sound of the telephone bell and the raised voice of my classmate to summon me. As the minutes and hours ticked by and no call came, I sank into despair. Slowly, I found ways to deal with these painful feelings.

If I stayed up all night reading and studying after I saw him when I still felt balanced, I found that I could sleep most of the day away. When I was awakened at twilight by his call, my life was delicious. When I woke up after dark to find that he hadn't called, the remaining hours before he might call again seemed less impossible to live through. I thought we were as close as any two people had ever been in the history of the world, but I never told him any of this.

During the summer, he went home to Boston and I went home to New York. We both had jobs. Leaving him was a new level of pain. My mind filled up with yearning like a lock with open gates. When we were apart, it felt as if I would never see him again, as if I had imagined him and he didn't really exist.

One of these painful Saturdays, I sat in my parents' living room pouring my heart out to my father, a man already working on his fourth or fifth scotch of the day. He knew how to help; he mixed me a strong gin and tonic, which had an amazing effect. Before the drink I had been sitting there in what felt like a prison of my own devising. I couldn't seem to make the man call, and I couldn't seem to bear that fact that he hadn't called. But as I sipped the gin and tonic, my fear and longing seemed to slip away. It was cool on the hot summer afternoon and I could almost smell the juniper taste mixing with the quinine taste of tonic as it went down. Outside, I could see a slice of the wrought-iron balcony between the house and the lawn; the afternoon shadows fell across the two birch trees on the other side of the brook. The Labrador that had been dozing at my feet shook herself awake and slammed out the screen door.

Quickly, my mood began to lift. What was I talking about with my father? It didn't matter; I could almost feel the squeeze around my heart easing up and the agitation in my stomach calming down. I loved a young man and he loved me, wasn't that wonderful? Weren't we lucky to have found each other? A few days apart, even a few weeks apart, were nothing to us, it suddenly seemed. The gin gave me courage. I was an amazing young woman sitting there looking out at the beautiful lawns of my father's house, I thought, and I was poised to have an amazing and adventurous life. There would be many men. There would be many interesting jobs and many drives back and forth to Boston to spend weekends with lovers. The pain I had been living with that had come to seem my most loyal companion just melted away as if it was a pile of sugar and the gin was water. I had another gin and tonic.

Soon enough, I discovered that drinking judiciously had another good result—it helped make me elusive and desirable. I used one obsession to control another; I was bargaining with chaos. I found that drinking to oblivion was a good way to bond with a man and a very good way to stop caring about whether or not he called. Getting drunk made men seem unimportant, and nursing hangovers was often a full-time job. I found that many men are excited by the idea of competing for a woman's affection, and so I tried to always be dating two or three men at a time. This came to seem normal and necessary.

tolerance and shame

One of the symptoms of addiction is what the experts call tolerance, the way in which it takes more and more of the substance each time to create the same result—this is the alcoholic's hollow leg. This ability and appetite, whether for sex, alcohol, or drugs, are often precursors of addiction. One of the horrible aspects of tolerance is that for a while an addict can achieve the same result that he or she gets at first, by using a larger amount of the drug or having more sexual partners, but there inevitably comes a time when no amount of the substance creates the result, and the addict is perpetually searching for a vanished high.

With desire this tolerance has a unique arc. After a while the love object—the person—stops engendering the high. The addiction turns, as addictions always do. At first, the more one sees the love object, the more compelling he or she becomes. Later, the more one sees the love object, the *less* compelling he or she becomes. Suddenly work, or family or sports seem fresh and compelling. In the case of sex addiction or even love addiction, this stage might seem to be a waning of the addiction. In fact, the addiction is becoming more powerful, so powerful that it is no longer satisfied with a particular person. The addict is enslaved by the feelings evoked by the person, not by the person in particular. The addiction is to the newness of the love experience, the opening gambits, the chase and the capture. Soon enough, the addict moves on to a new person in order to get the old feelings. The way people in twelve-step programs describe this is that they say they have a disease of *more*. Whatever feels good hooks them. If it's good, they want more of it. More and more.

The recovery bookstore is empty; it is almost always empty when I am there except for a woman buying a card or browsing the pink and green and radiant suns of the daily meditation bookshelf. Outside the store, which is tucked between a secondhand clothing store and a storefront decorator on a leafy block of the Upper East Side, it is raining. The store sells everything to do with recovery, from the coins that addicts give each other as congratulations at ninety days of recovery up to forty years of recovery, to books and tapes. Like almost everything in our world, twelve-step recovery has become an industry with its own profit centers and its own literature and even its own jewelry. Sex addiction books are selling well and steadily, ten or twenty or thirty a week, the store's owner tells me as I buy mine. None of them announce what they are on the cover—all have plain covers and many come wrapped in brown paper book jackets for good measure. A friend of mine who was a publisher's rep and went from store to store selling books from a catalogue once told me that his job gave him many, many sexual opportunities. There are four distinct twelve-step groups for dealing with sex addiction. This is unusual. There is one twelve-step group for three kinds of eating disorders—Overeaters Anonymous is also for anorexics and bulimics. There is one twelve-step group for alcoholics, which includes many drug users, one specifically for narcotics, and one for debtors. But four? Each of the four groups directed at recovery from sexual addiction has its own literature: Sex Addicts Anonymous, Sexaholics Anonymous, Sex and Love Addicts Anonymous and Sexual Compulsives Anonymous.

Why are there are so many different kinds of sex addiction twelve-step meetings? Is it because shame drives the addict away from identification? Sex addicts who think they don't belong in an established group because they are not that bad start a new group. Or perhaps it's so hard to feel safe in a sex addiction program that there have to be many. In meetings there is gravity and shyness that I haven't seen in other twelve-step programs; everyone is being very careful. On the online sites for these groups the notice that would tender a message of welcome on other recovery sites instead specifies who is *not* welcome. "If you represent the media, or you are a therapist, a student or you are just curious please let us know," reads the notice for S.A. in Manhattan. "We will have our members meet with you and speak to you. But you are not allowed in our meetings."

The books that I have bought to read about the subject— *Women Who Love Too Much; Sex Addiction; The Unsayable*—are so embarrassing that I don't keep them on my desk even though few visitors see where I work. I have hidden the research for this book in a drawer. I believe that this is an important book. We tell our young men and women that "falling in love" is the basis for building a life; it is not. Falling in love is a delicious, astonishing experience, but it has very little connection to the feelings and abilities two people need in order to build a life together and sustain a family. Falling in love is a wonderful, addictive, obsessive experience that usually lasts less than twenty months; the cases in which it leads to a happy, long marriage are often coincidental. When you fall in love, you should enjoy it for what it is—a brilliant roller-coaster ride, a dazzling sexual interlude, one of life's great experiences; you should not get married and have children, not until later when the addiction has passed and the person with whom you have fallen in love is revealed as a human being. I believe that if one or two people's lives were changed by the understanding of sexual behavior that I describe, this book would be worth writing. This is the book I wish I had read thirty years ago.

Yet the shame attached to this subject surrounds it like a thick, stinky fog. When people ask me what I am working on, I don't tell them. I tried for a while. "I'm working on a book about sex addiction," I said. Many people expressed their reaction with one negative word. The best responses were from those who assumed I was writing about Internet pornography. They asked about the statistics and the changes. I wanted to say to them no, I am not writing about Internet pornography; I am writing about *you*. My children have made me promise that this book will not be published until they are both away at college or living in other cities.

Patrick Carnes, who testified for Paula Jones and thinks that Bill Clinton's sex addiction moved public acknowledgment of sex addiction forward more than a decade, says "there is a deep ambivalence in our culture about sex. There is something in sex addiction to offend everyone."

One of the experts on addiction I interviewed, one of the most articulate of the dozens of people I spoke with, asked me not to use his name, so I'll call him X. In writing about him I will change some important details for reasons that will become clear. I have also changed key details for some of the other stories in this book, something which has never been necessary in all my years of writing nonfiction. X was a sex addict himself, a man with a penchant for younger women who seduced his way through a series of jobs, friends, and marriages. Nevertheless, his intelligence and talent, as well as his passion for the work, buoyed his career. He was a successful lawyer with a thriving practice. He represented famous men and women.

Slowly, he lost almost everything, and eventually, after he had stopped acting out sexually and began rebuilding his life and his career, he allowed himself to be interviewed by someone who was writing a series of articles about addiction. He told the writer everything, and the pieces that resulted from the interviews caused a sensation in the national magazine where they appeared. They won awards for the writer. X became an advocate for a new understanding of sex addiction. He became a poster boy for acknowledging addiction and recovering from addiction. His marriage disintegrated. His clients disappeared; he was threatened with disbarment in the state where he practiced.

Now, ten years later, this lawyer was willing to speak with me but only on the condition that I protect him. He has moved to another part of the country, practices a different kind of law, and is happily married again and the proud father of two young boys. He is in recovery from sex addiction. "I'll help you in any way I can," he said, "but you must not use my name."

X's story shows off the shame particular to sex addiction. If he had been an alcoholic or a drug addict, he could have joined the hordes of famous recovering alcohol and drug addicts who use their experience to proselytize recovery. Because his addiction was to other people instead of to heroin or cocaine, he was ostracized. Our world is rich with celebrity alcoholics and celebrity drug abusers, some in recovery and some still embarrassingly acting out. There are certainly many cases of famous, powerful, revered people acting out sexually. But it is rare to see a famous man or woman who publicly acknowledges their sex addiction and urges more understanding of his or her disease. We have seen many, many celebrity sex addicts, but when will we see a celebrity sex addict in recovery?

What is shame anyway? D. H. Lawrence wrote that he wished he could take off his shame as if it were a pair of shoes to leave on the porch. Isn't it just a fear of people and what they will think and what they will say? According to psychologist Paul Ekman in *Telling Lies: Clues to Deceit in the Marketplace, Politics, and Marriage,* "Shame is closely related to guilt, but there is a key qualitative difference. No audience is needed for feelings of guilt, no one else need know, for the guilty person is his own judge. Not so for shame. The humiliation of shame requires disapproval or ridicule by others. If no one ever learns of a misdeed there will be no shame, but there still might be guilt. Of course, there may be both. The distinction between shame and guilt is very important, since these two emotions may tear a person in opposite directions. The wish to relieve guilt may motivate a confession, but the wish to avoid the humiliation of shame may prevent it."

Somehow, perhaps because of this, shame seems to have more gravitas as a bad feeling than guilt. Is there an internal aspect to shame? Would we feel shame about something if we knew that no one would ever know? I'm not sure. If there is a conscience, and if we humans inherently know right from wrong, then the worst part of shame might be what happens when we turn on ourselves.

This conscience business is tricky though. Addicts do have a conscience; that's why one of the symptoms of addiction is remorse. The existence of a conscience is the difference between an addict and a sociopath or a psychopath: the psychopath has eliminated the difference between right and wrong; for the addict that difference is what makes addiction so profoundly painful. The addict does not want to act the way he or she acts. The addict promises repeatedly to stop. Yet the addict cannot stop.

When I tell people that I don't punish my children—I let their conscience administer the punishment because I believe that is far worse than anything I could do—they look askance. By punishing my children I take them off the hook. They have paid for their crime and can do it again. If I fail to punish them, they must answer to themselves. But if we punish children, it's because we assume their conscience isn't working. If we punish men and women and incarcerate them, it's because they seem to have demonstrated that they don't have a conscience. So as a culture we don't really seem to believe there is such a thing as a moral or ethical gyroscope in the human heart.

A few years ago I wrote a profile of then Westchester district attorney Jeannine Pirro. Pirro was as glamorous and beautifully dressed as she was effective. She was on fire for justice and usually brought down criminals all while wearing Armani suits and four inch heels. One case she prosecuted while I was following her around was that of a fifth-grade teacher who had molested two students. The students were being comforted and coached to testify, and Jeannine in her inimitable way was telling them how important it was for them to tell their stories on the stand. As the story unfolded, it became unbearably awful in many different ways.

The teacher had been at a New Year's Eve party at the home of the students and while at the party had become so drunk that he couldn't drive. When the students' father saw that the teacher had passed out at the wheel of his car before being able to turn the ignition key, he insisted that the teacher come back inside and sleep in the house. Sometime during the early morning hours, while everyone else was asleep, the teacher got up off the living room couch where he had been made comfortable and walked upstairs to the children's bedroom.

I told Jeannine that I thought the guy was an alcoholic and that he had probably been in a blackout. He wasn't lying when he said he didn't know what had happened; he probably had no memory of his own criminal actions. Jeannine replied that she knew the teacher was an alcoholic because he had previously been arrested for driving while intoxicated. He had been arrested more than once. I suggested that the man needed treatment as much as he needed incarceration. If untreated, I argued, his alcoholism would just reassert itself when he got out of jail and the same thing would happen again. He should go to jail, I agreed, but he should also go to rehab.

Jeannine expressed outrage at my suggestion as if I were somehow diminishing the man's disgusting crime or saying something that might cast aspersions on the children. "I have victims here!" she said, and turned away from me and walked away down the courtroom hall on her high heels.

Most of us first encounter addiction in a person close to us. Usually, it's an extremely painful encounter. Our husband has too much to drink at a party and disappears with the hostess for a little too long. When we confront him the next day, he is defensive but seems as confused as anyone about his behavior. Our son can't seem to pry himself away from the computer to do his homework, and his grades plummet. When we take away his computer, he enlists a friend to lend him one secretly. Our mother is dying of cancer, but she doesn't seem to be able to stop smoking. When we visit her on a bad day as she's lying in bed coughing, we look in her drawer and see a crushed pack of cigarettes. A wife, after being forgiven for a brief affair on a business trip, seems to have the same distracted air again. The telephone rings and there is no one on the other end of the line.

Quite recently, these behaviors were viewed as moral lapses. There was something wrong with the person's self-control. It seemed quite clear that if someone loved you they would not cheat on you. What could be more obvious than that a cancer victim should quit smoking? How could she continue to smoke when she knew it was killing her and adding misery to her last days? There has been a huge amount of education on the subject of addiction in the past ten years. The American Medical Association lists alcoholism and drug addiction as diseases. Treatments for all addictions focus on education, community, and the development of faith in some kind of higher power; they do not focus on self-control. Still, there is a resistance to the idea that an addict is helpless; at heart, many people still seem to believe that addiction is not a disease but a weakness. This is one of many sources of the shame that is an almost inevitable symptom of addiction.

"Sexual addicts are those who engage in persistent and escalating patterns of sexual behavior acted out despite increasingly negative consequences to self and others," writes Roschbeth Ewald in an essay on sexual addiction that cites Sandy Knauer's 2002 book *Recovering from Sexual Abuse, Addictions, and Compulsive Behaviors.* "They become addicted to the neuro-chemical changes that take place in the body during sexual behavior. To be seen as an addict is to be seen as inferior or defective. Usually an addicted person is considered weak or lazy."

* * *

The book *Addiction and Recovery for Dummies* tells me that sex addiction is especially painful because healthy sex is a way of being loving. "When unhealthy, this remarkable vehicle for intimacy makes a U-turn, and sex becomes antisocial, trust destroying, and isolating." The car metaphor is a stretch but I like the idea of a U-turn. Then the book says that sex addicts may find themselves in a cycle of sex addiction that begins with *preoccupation*—a trance state—and proceeds to *ritualization* and *compulsive sexuality*. This cycle and its description are already described in a similar way in Patrick Carnes's book *Out of the Shadows*. Carnes, however, includes a fourth stage of the cycle—*despair*. He defines sex addiction by comparing it with other addictions. He has come up with a simple description: "a common definition of alcoholism or drug dependency is that a person has a pathological relationship with a mood-altering chemical," he writes. The alcoholic's relationship to alcohol progresses "to the point where alcohol is necessary to feel normal."

Carnes divides addicts into levels of severity, but he divides them by what they do, not by how they do it. The mildest form of addiction in his definition is masturbation, and the most severe is patronizing prostitutes and cruising for casual sexual encounters. He also has sections on child molestation, rape, and violence. He makes the point that addiction rarely stays at one level. People who might think that they are safe because they only occasionally spend a night with a stranger or a few hours watching pornography are almost certain to have needs that escalate until their sexual acting out is at the center of life.

adultery

Adultery is the drunk driving of sex addiction. It is possible that someone who is not an alcoholic might get behind the wheel of a car after having had a few drinks, but it is improbable. Similarly, it is possible that someone who is not a sex addict or someone who does not have addictive propensities when it comes to sex might find themselves repeatedly committing adultery, but it is quite unlikely. By committing adultery we often break more than one promise.

At a Fourth of July party I sit next to another writer in a garden on the terrace of a building on Park Avenue where mutual friends have an apartment. She's a pretty, slender woman named Amy who I have known for a long time and who has written prize-winning books about politics and the economy. Since I am afraid to ask what she is working on, and I have a limited understanding of the federal banking system, I talk to her about what I am working on—a book about desire and addiction. I describe the addictive trance, and as I do, I can see her responding. The food is served buffet style, and we have both helped ourselves to salads and are eating propped against a huge ceramic planter seated on green-and-white-striped cushions.

As we eat, she tells me a story—all the while saying she can't believe she is telling me—about sleeping with a man who was married to a close friend while the close friend was at tennis camp. She remembers that it was as if she were in a trance. She had dinner with the man and told herself that of course that was okay just to have dinner with him. He took her to a romantic, expensive restaurant and she told herself that was because they both cared about food. She wore strappy high-heeled shoes because, she told herself, she wanted her friend's husband to feel that she wasn't having dinner with him only because of her closeness to her friend. She knew that she wouldn't sleep with him; he was the husband of her friend, after all.

She remembers the experience vividly and she especially remembers the way it seemed to be happening to someone else. As he took her home and went upstairs to her bedroom, she felt that she was in some kind of parallel universe where the normal rules didn't apply, some kind of dreamworld that only happened to have people in it from the real world. She remembers slipping her feet out of the shoes and then a few images. The next morning she almost thought it hadn't happened because it was so impossible. For three weeks afterward she couldn't stop thinking about him, but she kept herself from communicating with him in any way and the obsession passed.

Good marriages are based on a series of sexual promises being kept; adultery threatens marriage in more than one way. "The

major causes of marital dissolution worldwide are those that histor-
ically caused damage to the reproductive success of one spouse by
imposing reproductive costs and interfering with preferred mating
strategies," writes David Buss in *The Evolution of Desire*. "The most
damaging events and changes are infidelity, which can reduce a
husband's confidence in paternity and can deprive a wife of some or
all of a husband's resources; infertility, which renders a couple
childless; sexual withdrawal, which deprives a husband of access to
a wife's reproductive value or signals to a wife that he is channeling
his resources elsewhere; a man's failure to provide economic support, which deprives a woman of the reproductively relevant resources inherent in her initial choice of a mate; a man's acquisition
of additional wives, which diverts resources from a particular
spouse; and unkindness, which signals abuse, defection, affairs, and
an unwillingness or inability to engage in the formation of a coop-
erative alliance."

About twenty years ago I decided to write a book about adultery.
I thought I knew a lot about it from personal experience. I advertised
in the *New York Review of Books* and *New York Magazine* for people
who were committing adultery. I expected letters from people who
felt guilty about their cheating but were sometimes powerless to stop
it. I saw us as a potential band of sisters and brothers: sexual infidels
who were at once ashamed and proud of their behavior and who
would be joined together by their secrets. Instead I got letters from
angry men and women whose spouses had cheated on them.

Adultery fascinated and horrified me. Why couldn't I stop?
The addictive trance turned me stupid. Later, I felt a combination
of remorse, disbelief, and rationalization. I tried to give myself ex-
cuses. My husband did this and that, I told myself. He didn't take
out the trash, he never did the dishes, he was often depressed—
whatever it was—so of course I had to cheat on him. He was mean;

I needed more love than he could give me; et cetera, et cetera, et cetera. How could I have done such a thing? It must have been someone else's fault.

Ultimately, in order to stop sleeping with men I had decided not to sleep with, I actually had to stop talking with them. I had to draw the line so close to myself that I essentially gave up almost any contact with married men. I didn't have lunch with married men; I didn't chat with them on the phone, and I didn't answer their letters. If I had business with a married man, I only saw him during the daylight hours. I also had to stop drinking.

"Forrest and I sip Manhattans in the bar in the Ritz-Carlton," Sue William Silverman writes of the beginning of an affair she had with a married writer when she was a student. "He wears a tweed jacket with the maroon cashmere scarf draped over his shoulders. The flame of the white candle wavers as he speaks. It is hypnotic. Just like his voice. My mind fades. I seem to fade. . . ."

But it didn't always take a drink to make adultery irresistible. The last time I came close was about ten years ago. I was writing about a famous architect, and an editor asked me to interview him and go to see a house he had built in East Hampton. He and his wife were good friends of the editor. Warren and I had also been to dinner with the editor; on the day of this trip to East Hampton, Warren was in San Francisco where he often had to go for work or, as I came to suspect, just because he felt more comfortable there. After a few calls the architect said he would pick me up and drive me out to East Hampton from the city so that we could chat on the way.

There is something sexual about the enclosed space of a car. We laughed a lot on the way out, and the house was amazing, a showcase for his sexy, whimsical work. It was all very professional until the moment it wasn't.

Over pizza before driving back into town, he said something and I responded and it was as if we stepped into another country. Driving back into town, our conversation had a new dimension. It felt like laughing gas or dopamine had been pumped into the car. I couldn't keep myself from leaning over to touch him as we chatted. I imagined us in a motel room bed off the Long Island Expressway so vividly that it almost seemed to have happened. The car felt warm, my skin tingled.

Desperate for a way to stop this familiar slide, I began talking about my children, my love for Warren, our dog's health issues, anything I could find that seemed to dissipate the glow that now surrounded us. And it worked. Slowly, the eroticism seemed to ebb. The dopamine subsided. The urgency passed. When he dropped me off at my apartment house, I managed to escape with a kiss. Then he wrote me beautiful, sexy letters. I didn't answer them.

Although Warren and I were married to other people when we began our affair back in 1972, it didn't feel like adultery. We weren't breaking our promises, we told each other, we were responding to some higher promise. When I remember our times together over the last thirty-five years, we are always talking, furiously talking. We shared a fascination with newspapers—we had both spent years working for papers in the days of composing rooms and lead type—and we spent hours talking about reporting stories and structuring leads and different fonts and typefaces. We both had the habit of writing in our heads before we committed anything to paper; we could spend hours discussing the pros and cons of a lead or a subject. When he spoke about my work, Warren had a clarity and directness that I have never found anywhere else. He loved to say things that other people didn't dare say, including the word "fuck" used as a verb, noun, and adjective. He said that his friends Malachy and Frank McCourt wrote a play in which all the dialogue consisted of one word—"fuck"—delivered with a variety of inflections that advanced the narrative.

Once when I was at *Newsweek,* I had spent all day on a story about an editor named John Mack Carter. I had interviewed Carter and talked to his friends, and I proudly turned the story into the copy desk at about midnight and took a copy home to Warren. Warren read it as I took off my shoes and poured a glass of wine.

"I wouldn't print this," he said. I was horrified. What was wrong? Warren showed me that I had used unattributed quotes to make a point, something responsible reporters never do. He then explained why my lead was meaningless, the real beginning of the story was in the middle. "You can't turn this in," he said. I put my shoes back on and we took a cab downtown to *Newsweek,* signed in with the sleepy guard in the lobby, and retrieved the story from the copy desk. Back in my office on the darkened twelfth-floor hallway, I went through my notes and the clips to find quotes I could attribute. Warren leaned over the typewriter as I rewrote and restructured. This somehow felt more intimate than sex. He replaced adjectives and helped me find stronger nouns. He made cuts. Dawn was breaking as we put the new story back on the copy desk and headed uptown on Madison Avenue.

In the mid-seventies, when I was working at *Newsweek,* it seemed for a while as if the sexual freedom provided by the birth control pill and the liberations of the sixties were going to make women and men equal when it came to sex. The old ideas—that all women had something that all men wanted, and that by giving in women were dissipating their own power—seemed antique and stupid. Everyone liked sex. Sex was a great way to get to know someone. Why should women be any different than men? Warren agreed with me.

One night, I sat down next to an attractive man on the sofa at a party. He worked at a rival publication and this excited me. He was short with straight hair and bright blue eyes, but as I sank into the cushions, I realized that he was wearing some kind of cologne, and at first the smell of the cologne—Canoe, he said—made it hard for me to lean in to flirt with him. As the evening wore on, the cologne began to seem weirdly compelling. What had been a turnoff became a turn-on. The smell, with its woody, sweet overtones, began to overpower me as we sat closer and closer. The more I drank, the better it smelled. After a while, we left the party and went to my apartment. By the time we got into bed together, we were both quite drunk, and my small bedroom seemed to fill up with the smell of Canoe, which flooded the space.

I woke up with a headache, as well as the cotton mouth and disturbed stomach of a bad hangover. I had forgotten to lower the shades, and morning sunlight streamed mercilessly into the room onto the tangled sheets, which reeked of Canoe, and on the man who seemed much older and seedier than he had in the romantic dim light of the night before. When I got out of bed to make coffee, he woke up. He seemed surprised to see me and to find himself in my bedroom. He put on his rumpled clothes, tied his shoes, and, after an obligatory promise to get in touch soon, left. I took a long shower and thought I could chalk the whole thing up to experience, but when I stepped out of the bathroom, the smell of Canoe was still there; in fact, it seemed even stronger.

It was an early March day, and I opened all the windows in my apartment to let in the chilly air, but the smell just seemed to be activated by oxygen. I stripped the bed of sheets and the mattress pad, found an old fan, and turned it on and headed for the laundry machines in the basement of my building. There I turned the machines onto their highest settings and sat there, my head still spinning in time to the washing machine's turns, waiting for the sheets to wash and then dry. Remaking my bed with the laundered sheets, I still smelled the cologne, which seemed to have penetrated everything in my apartment. It took a long time for the smell to fade.

part two

what causes it?

repetition

"Although some see me as an 'expert' on trauma, I'm not," writes Annie Rogers in her book about working with traumatized young girls, *The Unsayable*. "Trauma is bigger than expertise of any sort— it's in our midst, in our language, our wars, even the ways we try to love, repeating, repeating."

As adults, we all seem to be drawn to the damage of our childhood. The sins of the fathers do set their sons' teeth on edge even after tens of thousands of dollars' worth of therapy. Something mysterious draws us back to those early days and nights, those days and nights when we had no way to judge our own experience and so it seemed like the whole world. If we grew up in a parochial small town where our differences were mocked, we may move to a big city to get away from that environment, only to discover the circumstances of the small town repeated in our apartment building

or in the community of our children's school. If we were molested
as children by someone close to us—and most molesters are family
members or family friends or members of the same community—
we can become prisoner to a sexual acting out in which someone
repeats some form of the molestation. If we were violated, we get
violated. If we were hit, we hit and get hit. If our parents divorced,
we inflict divorce on our children. Or we refuse to divorce and inflict a violent, erosive marriage on our children. Somehow, no
matter what our intentions, a kind of emotional gravity seems to
draw us back into the dark places of and before memory. How can
we resist that pull? Life's excitement comes from "our sense that
things are really being decided from one moment to another, and
that it is not the dull rattling of a chain that was forged innumerable ages ago," as William James wrote in 1890 of the way in which
we deal with the past.

 I live two blocks from where I went to kindergarten. When I
walk the dog, we trot along the East River on the walkway where
my father walked me to school before we moved to the suburbs in
the 1950s. In the narrow river, currents boil and suck at the Circle
Line Boats crowded with tourists gaping at our famous island, at
huge tankers from foreign ports whose sides seem to scrape the
high banks, at white police boats zooming toward the United Nations and trim yachts heading south from Long Island Sound. The
furious East River tides, named Sputen Duyvil, the spitting devil,
by the Dutch, rush down toward New York Harbor and the sea,
carrying everything with them; then a few hours later they surge
back the other way under the Hell Gate Bridge up through the
Harlem Ship Canal and to the Hudson River and on toward
Albany. My running route takes me past the playground where my
father taught me to roller-skate and under the Queensborough
Bridge, whose noise bothered my mother so much that we eventu-

ally moved. My brother was four when we moved; he lives out there in the suburbs a few miles from the house where he grew up.

The geometry of the soul is mysterious and implacable. Statistics show that women who have been in an abusive relationship are much more likely to get into another abusive relationship than other women. Almost 40 percent of women who are raped have been raped before. Being abused sexually as a child makes someone almost twice as likely to be abused as an adult. Being sexually abused as an adult also makes sexual abuse again much more likely. Reenactment, or the tendency of those who have been damaged to re-create the circumstances of the damage, is one of the most fascinating aspects of trauma. Statistics show an eerie shadow of trauma in the lives of those who have been abused.

"The adult survivor is at great risk of repeated victimization in adult life," writes Dr. Judith Herman in her classic, brilliant study *Trauma and Recovery: The Aftermath of Violence—from Domestic Abuse to Political Terror.*

Cautioning against blaming the victim or drawing the conclusion that somehow victims "ask for" abuse, Herman cites the statistics which show that two-thirds of women who were abused in childhood are subsequently raped, and other studies that document the high risk of rape and battering for women who have been previously raped and battered. "The phenomenon of repeated victimization, indisputably real, calls for great care in interpretation," Herman points out.

All addictions are based on repeating behavior. The essence of addiction is repetition, the doing over and over of the same thing. People in recovery say that insanity can be defined as taking the same action over and over and, each time, expecting different results. This is addictive insanity of course, but at the heart of all addiction is this recurrence of behavior or even—as in the case with victims of child abuse—recurrence of what looks like destiny. One of the devious things about this addictive repetition is the way the person destined to do the repeating is often blind to the pattern.

Where is the line between what is voluntary and what is involuntary? This is one of the puzzles of addiction, and it is also one of the puzzles of these statistics showing that abuse seems to perpetuate itself. Part of our culture's blindness to addiction—and we are so very blind—is because we seem unable to grasp the idea that people can be controlled by forces over which they have no conscious power. This is what used to be called fate. Now we know better. Not everyone has to keep an appointment in Samara.

Once addiction is identified, fate can sometimes be reversed. People who were destined to be alcoholics and die of alcoholism can seek treatment and stop drinking. Men who were fated to find new women irresistible can find help and change their ways. Addiction is a disease that can be treated. Although there are few believable statistics about addiction treatment—partly because some of the best treatment is through fellowships that ask members to remain anonymous— there are millions of people who testify that they are in remission from the disease of addiction. Treatment works. This is what Alcoholics Anonymous cofounder Bill Wilson called "a change of heart."

Dr. Herman, a Harvard-educated physician who teaches at Harvard Medical School and who runs a center at Cambridge Hospital for those who have been traumatized, is eloquent about the ways in which childhood abuse distorts the human soul or "deforms the personality," as she writes. "The child trapped in an abusive environment is faced with the formidable tasks of adaptation. She must find a way to preserve a sense of trust in people who are untrustworthy, safety in a situation that is unsafe, control in a situation that is terrifyingly unpredictable, power in a situation of helplessness."

There are as many different ways for the abused child to adapt as there are types of abuse, but the child and the adult he or she becomes has lost their sense of trust in other people and comfort in the world; this is a sense that is nurtured in more normal children. Herman discusses the severe difficulties in adaptation for those who have been traumatized.

One of the ways that these "deformed personalities" find to feel the comfort in the world that has been eroded is through addiction. Once a sex addict has discovered that having sex or being involved in an erotic relationship—either as the hunter or the hunted, the predator or the prey—can make him or her feel comfortable if only for a brief time, that addiction has begun. In a way, addiction replaces what trauma destroys, whether it is the soothing comfort that comes from the first few drinks, the relief of the first drug high, or the warm release of sex.

As Herman points out, many women before the 1970s were trapped in domestic lives that had the same psychological effect on them as combat had for soldiers in the field. "Women were silenced by fear and shame, and the silence of women gave form to every form of sexual and domestic exploitation," she writes.

However it happens, abuse has the same effect. Whether a man or woman inherits the distrust of the abuser from a parent or is directly abused, whether the deformed personality comes from being abused or watching as someone else is abused, abuse separates its victims from everyone else. The victims feel that they are alone in the world. They don't know what to do to be part of the human race. Everyone else seems to have an instruction book.

When abused adults search for feelings of comfort through

addictive behavior, sex is often a revelation for them. Those who have been unable to trust other people suddenly find a way to feel comfortable and trusting that actually involves other people. The addict who uses alcohol or drugs can become a loner, while the sex addict becomes social. Sex addiction and the emotional clouds that follow and precede it are the natural addiction for men and women who have lost their ability to trust others and who have seen through the humdrum texture of our lives into the evil dark places just below the surface. Trauma often feels as if it reveals some essential truth to which everyone else is blind.

In order to function as members of society, as individuals in a community, we have to act as if we believe—we have to believe—that most people are trustworthy. We have to expect them to stop at red lights and wait in line and teach our children well and leave us alone when we ask them to. Trauma shatters these illusions. The victim of a rape or an attack is physically injured, but the psychological injury is much greater.

I was mugged once by a man who broke in to the house where I was staying. I was living there with a man, of course, but he had gone on a daylong errand. It was the middle of the morning. I had been reading, and when I got up to take a shower, I heard windows and doors banging. I told myself it was the wind, but when I got out of the shower I found a man in my bedroom. He attacked me; I screamed and fought him off. I escaped being raped or murdered. I told myself that I was lucky. I ignored the psychic injury, and my psyche took decades to heal, if it ever really did. I will never again be unafraid in the way I was before the attack. I will always know how a few moments can change everything and catapult me into a nightmare. After the attack my search for comfort, for the moments of oblivion addiction provides, became more desperate. My friends who were *not* always afraid seemed stupid. I drank more, went deeper into debt, and reached out more feverishly for men.

Dr. Herman adds that "these distortions are not easily correctable by experience, since the survivor tends to lack the verbal and social skills for resolving conflict. Thus the survivor develops a pattern of intense, unstable relationships, repeatedly enacting dramas of rescue, injustice and betrayal."

Dr. Herman invites me for tea. I had e-mailed her my admiration for her book, a book that seemed to speak directly to me from its opening words. "The ordinary response to atrocities is to banish them from consciousness. Certain violations of the social compact are too terrible to utter aloud: this is the meaning of the word unspeakable. . . . Atrocities however refuse to be buried."

I have a romantic view of Cambridge and Harvard, e.e. cummings notwithstanding; "the Cambridge ladies live in furnished souls," he wrote. During the four years I was at Brown, I wished I were at Harvard; I spent a lot of time in Cambridge and audited some classes. I also spent two summers going to Harvard; later I went to a series of parties when the university gave my father an honorary degree there in 1978. My father's family comes from Boston, and Harvard somehow epitomizes the social and economic levels we were unable to achieve. Now that my daughter has been a graduate student at Harvard, I know that many people feel this romantic way about the place even when they are actually there. Its leafy ivory-tower feeling, its hushed sanctuaries and atmosphere of intellectual high-mindedness, always leave me wanting more.

I had imagined my tea with Dr. Herman taking place in a sunny parlor off Brattle Street, and Lapsang Souchong being served out of Spode teacups, but instead the appointed day was cold, windy, and overcast, and I got lost in the spiderweb of Cambridge streets near the Somerville line. Cambridge has streets of wooden mansions and great trees with grass sloping down to the street; Somerville has rows of pastel asphalt–sided houses with stoops rising from the pavement.

I had a map and directions, but I circled looking for the right street as the time for my appointment with Dr. Herman came and went. Cars behind me on Kirkland Street honked as I slowed to look at street signs. Everyone else was in a hurry and absolutely certain about where they were going. Dr. Herman had suggested that I might be coming by taxi, and now I saw why. I frantically juggled the map, the directions, and my reading glasses while trying to drive.

Finally, I passed a small alley with a sign marking it as Myrtle Street, and I remembered that Myrtle Street was close to Dr. Herman's house on the map. I made a sharp right and was catapulted into another world, a quiet hidden square of wooden houses fronting the street. I rang the doorbell and Dr. Herman directed me to the second floor of one of the wooden houses. Her kitchen was simple and cozy, the kitchen of someone who had better things to do than have the walls painted pale yellow and decorate with chintz. We drank tea out of heavy mugs.

Dr. Herman agreed that trauma is a cause of addiction, and she was also skeptical about the possibility of a pill to counteract addiction being discovered anytime soon.

"The conflict between the will to deny horrible events and the will to proclaim them aloud is the central dialectic of psychological trauma," she writes. I sipped tea and chatted about sex addiction and repetition compulsions of people who have been abused. "Adults as well as children often feel impelled to re-create the moment of terror, either in literal or in disguised form. Sometimes people reenact the traumatic moment with a fantasy of changing the outcome of the dangerous encounter. In their attempts to undo the traumatic moment, survivors may even put themselves at risk of further harm."

Dr. Herman told me about a study she had read done of men who were stranded on a North Sea oil rig when it sank. Half were drowned and the other half were clearly at risk for posttraumatic stress disorder, PTSD. Knowing this, they were told two things: one, talk about your experience and what happened, and two, resist the temptation to increase your drinking. These words of advice were printed on a card which each man got. It looked just like a membership card. Through these simple steps, most of the survivors of the disaster apparently avoided PTSD.

Dr. Herman and I sat at the round kitchen table and talked about the way abusers seduce their victims in the first place, how it starts. For a moment, she acted out the part of the abuser, suddenly animated, leaning over the table toward an imaginary victim. "You are special, what we have is special . . . no one else can know," she said, dropping into a weirdly menacing deeper voice. "This is our secret, you are chosen to share this secret," she hissed softly. Suddenly, the room was filled with her compelling voice. We were two distinguished women sitting safely at a kitchen table in Cambridge drinking out of pretty blue and white mugs, but my skin prickled with gooseflesh as I listened. I thought about the Old Testament: *The serpent is more subtle than any beast of the field.* Suddenly, I realized that I had left the front door open downstairs in my rush to get here on time. I could hear it banging in the wind. I was too uncomfortable to mention it.

As I prepared to leave, the telephone rang. It seemed to be Dr. Herman's husband; they discussed what to have for dinner. Again her voice lowered, but this time to a loving murmur.

the body

Addiction can be caused by at least three things. It can be passed down from generation to generation through the genetic makeup of each individual. There is definitely a genetic component to the tendency to choose infatuation over the possibility of long-term connection. Addicts also create families in which addiction seems to swirl in the air. NIDA director Dr. Nora Volkow says twin and family studies show that about 50 percent of addiction is genetic. Brain studies show that the developing brains of children of alcoholics are subtly different from the brains of normal children. These children are at risk for addiction just as the children of parents with certain kinds of cancers or diabetes or heart problems are at risk for those diseases. "But if you are never exposed to illegal drugs," Volkow says, "or if you grow up and live in an environment without trauma or too many stressors, you probably won't become addicted."

The genetic legacy of addiction is often confusing, as is the legacy for other diseases. People who are at risk of diabetes don't always get diabetes, for instance. A combination of environment and their genetic code creates the actuality of the disease. All addictions—alcoholism, eating disorders, sex addiction, even the codependency of a nonalcoholic born into a family of alcoholics—seem to be mixed up in the genetic grab bag. A couple who have alcoholism and bulimia between them may have one child who is a sex addict, one child who is a drug addict, and one child who is perfectly fine. Two drug addicts will have a daughter with anorexia or a son who can't seem to keep track of money. Addiction can move sideways—some alcoholics have addiction-free parents and addicted aunts or uncles—or it can skip a generation, causing grandchildren to act out in ways that may baffle their parents, until they remember clues from their own early childhoods.

In addition to the genetic component, addiction can also be fostered or discouraged by the environment in which one lives. Certain environments—the barracks of soldiers who have taken a pledge not to drink, for instance—make it almost impossible to drink, and people in those environments more rarely become drunks. Some organizations and religions require a pledge of sobriety as a prerequisite for membership, while others depend on the kind of connections that are fostered by drink. A man or woman who lives in a small community where sex is actively discouraged will be less likely to act out in an addictive way than someone growing up in a bordello.

Recently, a few psychologists and writers have expanded an idea about trauma and addiction that explains a lot—the idea that trauma and emotional damage is held physically in the human body.

In her fascinating book *Secrets, Lies, Betrayals: How the Body Holds the Secrets of a Life, and How to Unlock Them,* the Yale University writer and psychologist Maggie Scarf interviews a series of women who seem enmeshed in bad situations, situations that they have the tools to think their way out of rationally. Nevertheless, they are paralyzed, or eager to please a man who is clearly manipulative. Her hypothesis, supported by a great deal of research, is that when a child is damaged or even when a child is delighted, the feelings enter the body and that the response is physical rather than emotional. This is why therapy which relies on talking is limited. "The basic theme of this book is, in a phrase, that the body knows more about our experiences—about the things that have happened to us in our lives—than words can possibly express," Scarf writes. "... While we usually think of our emotional lives as being psychological in nature, they are in fact *deeply rooted in our bodily experiences* of charged events that are occurring or have occurred in the past."

To undo this kind of damage, the body needs to be freed through exercise or physical manipulation. It's the body, not the mind, that needs to be healed. The body knows the score. "There are innumerable life situations in which our bodies are sending out somatic cues, signals and announcements—'Something's feeling "off" here' or 'I'm not sure this person can be trusted'—but transmitting this information in the form of vague physical discomforts or minor symptoms rather than through the more precise medium of thoughts and language. These body-based data contain vital information and need to be attended to on a routine basis, translated from the crude physiological signals ('My stomach is in knots') into important bulletins that can at times be crucial to the whole person's well-being."

In other words, the body acts almost on its own in response to a series of physical cues the mind may not even be aware of. We're schooled to screen out what the body is trying to tell us. Certainly, when it comes to sex addiction, it's the body, not the mind, that seems to be following commands from the past. "Why and how does it happen that our bodies can hold the knowledge of situations and events that we ourselves have forgotten?" Scarf asks. What happens is that the body is so busy responding to remembered threats that it loses its ability to respond sensibly to the present. "In the wake of overwhelming stress," Scarf writes, "a person is likely to feel profoundly unsafe and to see dangers and difficulties lurking everywhere. Curiously enough though, that same person is often credulous and unseeing when it comes to recognizing and identifying the realistic threats that do exist in his or her life." We all have physical symptoms of warning and distress: shallow breathing, speeded-up heart rate, a tight feeling in the stomach. In some people these warnings have been ignored so often that they are no longer noticed.

This idea, the idea that our addictions and damaging views of the world can be held physically, in our walk, in our body shape, in our facial expressions, or in the way we hold ourselves, and in our physical reactions is revolutionary, but it has roots in everything from L. Ron Hubbard's *Dianetics* to Dr. John Sarno's treatment of physical pain as a result of unacknowledged pain and rage in his brilliant book *The Mindbody Prescription*. Throughout history people have discovered and rediscovered the connection between the body and the spirit. In our secular world it is harder to believe than ever. If you are overweight, shouldn't you eat less? If you are in an abusive marriage, shouldn't you leave? If you have a physical ailment, shouldn't it require a physical cure? If you have an emotional or mental ailment, shouldn't it require an emotional or mental cure?

Especially when it comes to addiction, the body seems to be

acting out the mind's secret pain. The addict's trance state, the way in which the addict is taken over by the addiction so that he or she seems to be sleepwalking, is the body getting its own back. In this state promises and resolutions are not forgotten; they seem to be from another world. An addict in a trance state often realizes too late what has happened, but even then the addictive act—the sex with someone else's husband, the pornographic release—seems to have happened to someone else.

When I first met Maggie Scarf at a party twenty years ago, she told me a story about being trapped on a small airplane with my father flying from Boston to Maine. "He was the angriest man I ever met," she said. Most people don't talk that way about my father. She saw through the façade. We became friends.

This time Maggie Scarf and I meet up at the Frick Museum, an urban palace on Fifth Avenue that was once the home of Henry Clay Frick and which has for years housed an astonishing collection of paintings: Turners, Constables, De La Tours, and Fragonards in period rooms grouped around a central atrium with splashing fountains and a shallow pool. I came to the Frick often as a child, and when we moved to the suburbs, I would often take the train into Grand Central and walk up to the museum, which seemed to hold a special kind of serenity within its walls.

Maggie and I take in the Turners, two gorgeous paintings of harbors where the clouds of water seem to become the clouds of sky. I show her the Bellini painting of St. Francis that used to hold me transfixed. I would stand there transported far from the world around me until the museum guard would come and tell me it was time to close, and I had to take the train back to my miserable life as an unpopular suburban teenager.

Maggie has a kind of personal serenity herself and she has often helped me with writing. When I haven't known how to proceed or where to go next, her advice has been invaluable. Because she suggested it, I taught at Yale for a semester, and she worked on *Secrets, Lies, Betrayals* while in my class of talented undergrads. At the end of her book Maggie describes going through a process called EMDR, which is a way of actually reprogramming the body's physical responses.

Later, I talk with the therapist Patti Levin, who treated Maggie Scarf with EMDR. Levin believes that trauma is held in the body as well as the brain. She uses a method (eye movement desensitization and reprocessing), which relies on guided eye motions to unlock this kind of trauma.

"It's as if your brain was a filing cabinet and some things were misfiled," explains another friend, who went through EMDR after a startling weight gain following the traumatic death of a high school friend. "This is a way of breaking those destructive attachments and refiling things where they are meant to be."

Patti Levin is about to get married for the third time. Like some other therapists I have spoken with, she is open and interested when it comes to the subject of sex addiction. Of course, people don't experience shame about the behavior of their clients, so therapists are a group of people I'm delighted to interview.

Levin says that she has a patient who is a sex addict in pursuit of feeling pretty. "She feels ugly, and being with a man makes her feel pretty," she says. I understand that; many women don't feel pretty. But I think addiction is less specific than that. I think that "pretty" is really a code word for "desirable." Many people do not feel desirable, men and women. Addiction is one response to these painful feelings. People drink because that makes them feel desirable and at one with the world. Bill Wilson, the cofounder of Alcoholics Anonymous, had his first drink at a party, a party where he had felt like a social outcast before he had the drink. Before the drink he was cringing with discomfort; after the drink he was the life of the party. As he wrote, he had "found the elixir of life." Gamblers also gamble because standing at the table, winning, makes them feel powerful and desirable.

Levin says that she has often tried to send clients to S.L.A.A. (Sex and Love Addicts Anonymous) but that it doesn't seem to work in the same reliable way that Alcoholics Anonymous works for alcoholics. She says that her patients report that there are a lot of predators in the twelve-step rooms when it comes to sex addiction. I wonder what makes a predator. Is every man or woman looking for a sexual connection a predator?

I read Dr. Robert Katz's self-published journal about being a sex addict. After my reading in William James's *Varieties of Religious Experience*, it seems refreshingly direct. Katz does not mince words; he doesn't reach for the scholarly explanation when the vernacular will do. He writes about how he fucked this one and he fucked that one. His addiction was to the conquest and he never stayed with any woman for more than a few months. Even when he liked a woman and she diminished his loneliness, he found that he had to keep on conquering other women.

For him the driving force behind the addiction was loneliness, he writes. It was a loneliness so intense that when he sensed loneliness in the women he met, he fled as fast as possible. He saw the world as a seething mass of lonely women hungry for his ministrations. Each time he did get involved, he felt that he was helping the woman. He was no predator! After all, he was a doctor who had been to medical school and taken the Hippocratic oath.

It's a shocking book. He tells of the way some ob-gyns describe their pleasure at feeling women's breasts and vaginas. His gynecology professor tells him that when an ob-gyn palpates a woman's vagina for more than fifteen seconds that is "just playing."

Katz does look back into the loneliness of his childhood for answers. His book is also an identification of addiction as being about emotional intensity rather than specific activities. This kind of addiction hides in plain sight. This kind of addict doesn't do anything weird. He's not a flasher or a pederast or a Peeping Tom. He doesn't meet up with other dads in the grimy bathrooms of playgrounds for a quick suck while their children climb unattended on the jungle gyms or play in the sandbox. No, no. He does what everyone else does. He courts a woman and then sleeps with her. Sometimes he sleeps with the same woman for a long time. There is nothing eccentric about it. No one wears handcuffs or has anal sex with a gerbil or even uses any sex toys. His addiction is normalcy taken to a degree that makes it abnormal.

Where is the line between being a normal person and doing normal things—the seduction, the bedding, the intimacy (at least for a while)—and the addict who ends up with multiple partners and is unable to progress from sex to having a real connection with another human being? What's the difference between Dr. Katz, a self-described addict, and the men who cheat on their wives every time they go on a business trip, and get married two or three times, men whom our culture treats as being perfectly fine? Is there a certain number of sex partners that makes a man or woman an addict? If you've slept with five hundred people, are you automatically an addict? Fifty?

In addiction studies, since addiction is about intensity and amount rather than about specific activities, there are always going to be sharp questions about what constitutes addiction. In a way, this is the part of sex addiction that is most parallel to other addictions. Many people drink socially. Everyone eats and spends money.

Many people gamble every now and then. Which of them hide the potential for addiction? Which of them are already there?

In addictions identified by specific behaviors, it may be easier to trace the path of the traumas of the past. Adults who were molested as children often molest children. But the idea of the power of the past is relatively new. In the great literary classics about sexual yearning, many cut off this avenue of inquiry. Tolstoy tells us nothing about Anna's childhood or Flaubert about Emma's. It's the brilliance of Charlotte Brontë's *Jane Eyre* that the woman's childhood with its many traumas clearly matches up with her traumatic adulthood and her responses to that adulthood. Brontë was a seer. Her sister Emily, who wrote *Wuthering Heights,* one of the great addiction classics of all time, created characters who were unchanging from childhood to adulthood. By the time F. Scott Fitzgerald wrote about romantic obsession in *The Great Gatsby*—an obsession fueled, as many addictive obsessions are, by adversity—he knew enough to give Gatsby a past, a past that had required a complete self-invention the center of which was the right woman, Daisy Buchanan.

Perhaps the addictive trance state is a physical response, not an emotional or intellectual one. Addiction may be a disease of the brain, but it may be a disease triggered by other parts of the body: the sense of smell, a texture, a taste or feeling, a certain kind of motion or combination of visual cues. If trauma is held in the body, that would explain why it doesn't respond to intellectual or emotional triggers. You can decide with your mind and even your heart that you aren't going to sleep with him. But once you are in the same room, your body takes over, just the way the body takes over when it is hungry and food is presented, or the way it takes over when you are exhausted and lie down although you don't plan to sleep. The body has a mind of its own in many circumstances; addiction is one of those circumstances.

What provokes this physical response? How can the body go so completely out of control? Sometimes it may be a cue that the body receives to which the conscious mind is not alert. Is it a coincidence that the most addictive love affair of my life was with a smoker, a man who smelled just the way my father smelled when I was growing up? If the body is the culprit in addiction, the body as a single agent, then there is very little that psychiatry or understanding can do. The body itself has to be reprogrammed.

This is often part of what happens in twelve-step meetings. Addicts talk about the healing effect of hearing other people's stories and knowing that they are not alone. The physical requirement of twelve-step meetings—that the addict sit still and listen for an hour—may be as important in changing the addictive brain as anything else. Although there is no research or literature on the subject of the physical healing that goes on in meetings (partly because, of course, people in meetings are anonymous and can't be interviewed or studied in the normal way), anyone who regularly goes to a meeting can see it happening. In being forced to listen to other people's stories, the addict is pried away from the hot center of obsession and the possibility of acting out. There is no talking back or response—no cross talk, they say—and this means that, except for the few minutes the addict may be sharing his or her own story, the addict must sit more or less still. In this situation it is almost impossible to stay focused on one's own problems and one's own desires. Other people's stories bang on the door of the addiction. The body relaxes in a unique and pleasurable way. The heart slows. The mind calms. The body lets go.

old age is a new thing

One of the changes in our world in the last century that has fed sexual addiction is the extension of some life spans by more than thirty years. For the first time in human history we select few, we wealthy residents of wealthy countries, can expect to live another thirty years after middle age. This has an enormous effect on what our marriage vows mean and has made a significant change in our sexual attitudes and behaviors. When life was short and often cut off by illness or accidents, or in countries where life is still short (my life expectancy is eighty years; in some African countries, life expectancy is thirty-six years), marriage and sex have different meanings.

If your life expectancy is in the forties and you marry in your twenties, you barely have time to reproduce and send your children out into the world. It's not that adultery doesn't happen to young people, but a twenty-five-year-old who expects to live to be eighty will behave very differently from a twenty-five-year-old who expects to live to be forty. One of the great spurs to adultery is the idea that we are missing out on something. At the age of forty-three I was haunted by the idea that I was settling for a stable marriage when there were all kinds of fireworks, emotional and sexual bells and whistles, available to me. I was just reaching my prime, I thought. My career was going well, I was healthy and attractive. I hear other women say it too when they reach their forties. "Is this all there is? Am I going to have to settle for this? Am I winding down?"

Somehow, I was still looking at sex relations as some kind of game where the winner is the person who has collected the most: the most experience, the most husbands, the most delicious moments. My addiction made me restless, and the culture told me that it was wrong to accept less: less than I "deserved," less than I "had earned," whatever those phrases mean. I was supposed to overcome the low self-esteem fostered by the traumas of my childhood and open myself to the world. I was supposed to follow my bliss. But the world in which a woman can feel she has reached her prime in her early forties is really new. And a world in which a woman can still be sexually hungry in her early forties is even newer, a product both of the extension of our life expectancy and of the sexual liberations of the 1960s and 1970s.

This change has caused confusion in families at the same time that we have been propelled into the phenomenon of old age, the "senior moment" that goes on for decades. Not only does the family no longer serve its purpose in tending a family farm or contributing to the life of a village; the family and the marriage which is at the center of it now must survive an extra thirty years.

Now instead of dying, some of us have a new chapter to the

story of our lives, and that chapter—with all the freshness of a discovered thing, of a bonus, of gravy—is a chapter many people do not want to spend doing the same old same-old. Old age is a brand-new thing, and people want to spend it in new ways. Pills and plastic surgery keep them young enough to handle something new. New drugs and therapies keep them able to perform with the sexual vigor of much younger men and women.

From the beginning, Warren and I had partly dealt with the difficulties we faced by deciding to grow old together. Perhaps we couldn't spend time together at the moment—we had other obligations, many other obligations—but the day could come when we would be two old people with nothing better to do than sit around and talk. One response to the frustrations of the present was to imagine a different future.

We would end up, Warren always said, in a seedy English seaside boardinghouse in someplace like Tunbridge Wells in Kent. I had been in those little hotels with my first husband, the kinds of places where you eat thin broth in a dreary dining room with old-age pensioners sitting at two other tables and the waiters wishing you were done. Then the feeling that we were at the end of the earth had been depressing; now I wanted nothing more than to be there, at the end of the earth with Warren.

It was a fantasy, but somehow, Warren acquired the stationery of our imaginary seaside hotel, and every now and then I would get a letter on a pale blue piece of paper with a darker blue Tunbridge Wells Spa letterhead complete with telegraph address. I keep important papers, social security cards, passports and old love letters in an inlaid sewing box like the one in which my parents kept their important papers. Now I shuffle through the pile of birth certificates and locks of hair from my children's first haircut, teeth that had been taken from under pillows by the tooth

fairy, and a two-dollar bill. There are quite a few letters in Warren's loopy handwriting, and I open one from Tunbridge Wells
Spa. "Happy anniversary," it says, "I love you." It was written in
1974 and dated the day in July when we had first spent the night
together.

environment

Does availability diminish addiction? In the seventeen years between the night we met and the day we married, were Warren and I completely in love with each other, or were we also in love with the idea of our star-crossed situation, the idea of overcoming obstacles? When there are no adversities, is obsession more or less likely to take root? Does the Internet with its endless possible pornographic possibilities cause sex addiction, or does it mitigate addiction? Online, everything is available all the time. There are few obstacles. Yet the computer itself may be enough of an obstacle.

The question of the role of the Internet in the growth of sex addiction is a controversial one that already has its own television show, a series called *To Catch a Predator,* which aired last year. In three days the Internet sting set up by the program brought thirty-two men into a house in Long Beach, California; each of them had the expectation of having sex with a girl who said she was thirteen. There is something terrifying and weirdly fascinating about this show, which riveted the television-watching American public and even spawned its own book.

The "predator" is a man who has responded with sexually graphic e-mails online to a woman claiming to be underage and available. He arrives at a house, little realizing that his arrival is on camera. He knocks or rings and then agrees to wait in the kitchen while the girl, an actress, dries her hair. Then, suddenly, the show's host, Chris Hansen, confronts him.

Sometimes the predator is baffled and takes Hansen to be the girl's father. Inevitably the predator collapses into defenses and apologies. Hansen then bullies him. The audience is treated to a reality television dose of pure shame as the predator verbally twists in the wind. *I'm not a bad person,* he will mumble. Hansen then asks him if he sent a photo of his genitals to a thirteen-year-old girl, and he produces the photo or other incriminating e-mails and waves them around in front of the camera.

We're watching someone else's nightmare, and the fact that they are a person who wanted to do something repulsive and illegal seems to make it all right. There's a quality of lynching about it, although, God knows, in order to agree to meet a thirteen-year-old girl for the purpose of having sex, you would have to be an idiot— or an addict. Sometimes the men who get caught have even watched the show. In a few cases men who have already been caught, humiliated by Chris Hansen, and arrested by the local police and served time, return to get caught again and confronted by Chris Hansen again and arrested again. This is addiction in action. Neither Chris Hansen nor the men themselves seem to have any idea what's going on.

Larry King has Chris Hansen and John Walsh, another television host, on his show. They talk about the predators with distance and horror as if they were talking about a race of mutants. There is only black and white in the discussion: the children are innocent; the children's parents are innocent and concerned; the men who get caught are evil. No one mentions addiction. Larry King asks in wonderment how men who have actually seen the show could be dumb enough to get caught by the sting they have watched on their television sets, but he and Hansen shrug at this level of stupidity. "The drive is so strong that they are willing to risk it," Hansen tells King.

The really scary thing is not the predators and their numbers and their frequency, although they are indeed profoundly disturbing. The really scary thing is that jailing addicts doesn't work. When addicts get out of jail, they return to their old behavior. Addicts need to be changed as well as being incarcerated until they can change. That change comes through treatment. In this whole drama addiction is the invisible engine, the puppet master pulling the strings.

Probably one of the main things that viewers like about *To Catch a Predator* is reassurance that the danger to their daughters comes from outside, from strangers who stalk them on the Internet. On the contrary, most molesters and abusers are people who know the victim and are trusted by the victim's family. If the threat is online, parents imagine, their children can be protected by Internet filters and computer time limits and judicious spying. In the drama of *To Catch a Predator*, the predators drive up in cars and they are strangers; they are not teachers or brothers or uncles. The show distracts worried parents and children from the real threat because it depicts what trauma studies call "stranger danger," danger that is relatively easy to avoid.

The program also deals with addiction in a way that is deeply punishing. Would Hansen bully and harass a drunk the way he goes after the repulsive men who are caught in his net? Many television hosts make their ratings by bullying addicts; a typical week on Dr. Phil or any of the daytime judge shows features an addict, usually apologizing, being scolded by the show's host. This can be good entertainment, I guess, but addicts never heal through criticism, scolding, or bullying. When Dr. Phil or Judge Judy or Oprah tells a young man to get himself together and find help, they might as well be speaking in a foreign language.

What changes in our culture have created such an odd program as *To Catch a Predator*, with its heady combination of shame, prurient voyeurism and puritanical self-righteousness? It's a program so extreme that people who haven't seen it can hardly believe it exists. Our society has changed more in the past fifty years than in the preceding five hundred, especially when it comes to relations between the sexes. Marriage, for instance, as Helen Fisher points out, was originally an institution created to fit the needs of an agricultural society. Farmers need families; for generations the American way of sex has been tied to the creation of families.

Now, Fisher argues, we are shifting from being an agricultural society to being a nomadic society. In fact, our escalating emphasis on the importance of the wedding ceremony may be an act of panic. As marriage becomes actually less important as our culture shifts, we try to anchor ourselves to the past by making it more important.

The number of farmers has dropped precipitously in the last twenty years. People rarely live in one place for more than ten years. Few people live in the house where they were born or even the village where they were born. Our town centers are abandoned and our airports are mobbed. Our roads are clogged with traffic, real estate sales boom. And in a nomadic society, the family is more a hindrance than a help. Everyone moves faster on their own.

As the old family structure has disintegrated, as divorce has become common and life expectancy has increased, as our society has become more and more mobile, our culture has become particularly friendly to sexual promiscuity. The first hint of an illicit orgasm is available to any one in a hotel room through an extensive menu of pornography movies and channels. Families are far away; pleasure is in your face.

As the world changes, addictions seem to grow. "Our massive exposure to sexual stimulus has created a new generation that will be struggling with this for years," predicts Patrick Carnes. The Internet feeds addiction, he believes. The shift to a nomadic, anonymous society feeds it; the end of community feeds it.

Stanton Peele in his essay "Fools for Love" (collected in the anthology *The Psychology of Love,* edited by Yale psychologists Professor Robert Sternberg and Michael Barnes) explains the changes in our culture and the way they have fed love and sex addiction. As he points out, love is a lure in our culture, a promise of a rich, satisfying adulthood. For those who read serious literature, however, there are certainly warnings. "Why is great literature . . . so much more skeptical than contemporary social psychology of the attachments people form and give the name love to?" Peele asks.

Peele believes that there is a historical chain of events that has led to our society's emphasis on love and sex and which feeds our addiction and our blindness to that addiction. As families and communities have become smaller, he points out, marriage or the primary male-female relationship has become more important. Because of this pressure on marriage and its individual men and women, marriage itself has become stifling and intolerable, he writes. Our devotion to romantic ideals can be "dysfunctional and pathologic."

In fact, the American divorce rate, one of the highest on earth, has slightly declined in the last few years, but this statistic is misleading, as are many of the interpretations and reinterpretations of the census data and studies conducted by the Centers for Disease Control and Prevention on marriage and divorce. For instance, although the divorce rate has dropped about 5 percent since 1980, the marriage rate has dropped by close to 50 percent. Our country has the lowest percentage of children who grow up with both biological parents in the world.

Chasing an ideal of love, a love that is limiting in many different ways, shuts out the rest of society; love cannot take the place of extended families and communities. When a predator picks up a sixteen-year-old girl online and arranges to meet with her, he goes to jail. Yet when a captain of industry or a distinguished editor deflowers his young girlfriend in a hotel room on her eighteenth birthday and then leaves his wife for her, there is no jail time or even much shame. His circle of friends may not all embrace his new wife, but in our culture such a couple has little trouble reconstituting a supportive group of friends, family, and colleagues.

is sex addiction the male version
of female bulimia?

Dr. Martin Kafka, a clinical psychiatry professor at Harvard who has treated sex addicts for eighteen years at McLean Hospital in Belmont, Massachusetts, has his own definition of addiction in general and sex addiction in particular. "Paraphilia" is the word psychologists and doctors use for serious sexual disorders: in the *DSM-IV* this includes everything from pedophilia to an inability to have an orgasm. Dr. Kafka includes promiscuity, compulsive masturbation, telephone sex dependence, and cybersex. Disorders that don't quite qualify as paraphilia Dr. Kafka has classified as paraphilia-related disorders, or PRDs. This is his primary area of treatment.

Kafka started as an eating-disorders specialist at McLean

twenty years ago. In those days treatment for eating disorders was perfunctory, and the women being treated had to share a building with others being treated for a variety of mental illnesses and disorders. One day Dr. Kafka had a life-changing "eureka" moment. He noticed that while the bulimics he was treating for eating disorders were 95 percent women, the sex addicts were 95 percent men. Kafka realized that these bulimics and their hospital mates with PRDs were both suffering from a disregulation of appetite. "I began to think that the PRDs are to men what eating disorders are to women. I was so excited by this breakthrough, I didn't sleep for two nights," he told Lauren Slater for an essay in the *New York Times Magazine* in 2000. Once he began thinking about it, Kafka saw many other parallels between bulimia and PRDs. Both are physically violent and both end with a discharge of bodily fluids. He asked himself if vomiting or purging could be some kind of stand-in for a female orgasm.

The connection between the appetite problems of women with eating disorders and men with sex disorders also has chemical evidence from brain scans to support it. Kafka calls it the "monoamine hypothesis" because he is looking at the role that our monoamines—dopamine, norepinephrine, and serotonin—play in controlling appetite and mediating desire. Using drugs like Prozac or Celexa, which affect serotonin, Kafka has been successful in turning many men whose deviant sexual needs had ruined their lives into normal, loving husbands. One of his deviants described the overwhelming need he felt for sex as a wave. According to Kafka, in many of his patients these drugs have worked the miracle of wiping out deviance while leaving normal sexuality alone. Dr. Kafka does not treat his PDR patients as if they were addicts.

When I interview Dr. Kafka on the phone, he is eating lunch at his desk at McLean, and I am catching a moment on a book tour from a hotel room in Louisville, Kentucky. With the intensity of people on a desert island—those working with sex addiction feel so isolated that they have an instant bond—we begin to disagree. Kafka primarily treats men, and he thinks that sex addiction is different in men than in women; it's more "genital," he says. He points out that a male sex addict will masturbate when he can't find a woman—it's all about the orgasm. For a man, sexual addiction is the wish to have an orgasm. I'm not sure that's different for women, but I don't say much. This sounds to me like the old truism about men wanting sex and women wanting love; men wanting to get laid and women seeking attachment.

As Helen Fisher has pointed out, there seems to be a conspiracy among men and women to propagate the myth that men are more sexual than women are, that for men sex is less connected to feelings than it is for women. Men are supposed to commit adultery more than women do, but, Dr. Fisher says, "who are they committing it with if not women?" Statistics show that in fact men who lose their wives and are without long-term relationships don't do well, while women who lose their husbands appear to thrive.

When Dr. Kafka describes some of his patients, men and women, who are sexually preoccupied, they sound like the kind of addicts I'm writing about. They are people who may not notice for a long time that their sexual behavior is keeping them from forming real connections to other people, or that they are breaking promises they have made with increasing frequency.

When I finally bring the conversation around to addiction, I find that Dr. Kafka has his own definition of it: he thinks that addicts are people with underlying psychological conditions they are covering over by using a substance. Can it be this simple? We are sad and angry, depressed or upset, and so we seek out sex, compulsively, to change our moods. Addicts are "medicating underlying psychiatric problems," he says. Once the underlying psychiatric problem is treated, often with an antidepressant, the sex addict stops seeking out this damaging way of self-medicating and goes back to having a normal sex life.

Sex addiction is a source of tremendous shame for his patients, Dr. Kafka says, and that's because it is so destructive. In sex addiction "the rock bottom that keeps us caring about each other is compromised." The thing that matters most in this world—I would call it community—can't take place with an addict because the addict has to lie and cheat in order to continue.

I experience the shame of talking about sex and love addiction every time an audience member asks me what I am writing about. In Louisville they have come to hear me discuss a group biography I have written about Concord, Massachusetts, in the 1840s. During the question-and-answer time after my talk, someone asks about my next work. I lie. I am very good at lying. Although I rarely lie anymore, I am a charming liar who can make the person I'm lying to feel comfortable about what I am saying even though it isn't true. I imagine a wave of fascination and disgust that will emanate from this audience if I tell them the truth. Instead of saying that I am writing about sex addiction, I tell them that I am writing about the harmony and disharmony of human desire. They lose interest and go on to more questions about writing.

Dr. Kafka sends me his overview of this subject, and I am plunged into the knotty language of psychologists. In his paper Dr. Kafka defines PRDs as "disinhibited or exaggerated expressions of human sexual arousal and appetites." In other words, *too much sex.* The first symptom of PRDs in Dr. Kafka's analysis is that the patient is isolated by secrets. "PRD behaviors are secretive because they engender considerably more shame, guilt, and blame than other sexual disorders."

Dr. Kafka's second point is that "most subjects" with PRDs have something else wrong with them: "multiple lifetime comorbid mood, anxiety, psychoactive substance abuse and other . . . diagnoses." Teasing meanings out of the dense language of the study, I find that the section called "comorbidity with other sexual disorders" describes the waning of sexual arousal "especially when the initial infatuation phase of the relationship has passed." This is an aspect on which all agree, for different reasons.

Dr. Fisher, in describing this waning of sexual desire and the resulting spike in the divorce rate at three and four years, argues that women are genetically programmed to seek a series of mates in order to increase their chances of having healthy children. In the addiction model the waning of desire is part of the mechanics of addiction. The addict is not addicted to one person in spite of the fact that during the most intense phases of addiction this is how it feels. In sex addiction, change does what increased quantity does in some other addictions. The alcoholic switches to martinis, the sex addict needs a new partner.

all of the above

Love and sex seem to be the parents of a thousand theories. Many people who have been through the wild, irrational moments caused by love have found a small measure of comfort in spinning rational ideas about what happened to them. This is how we always explain what we can't explain, from the stories told about the constellations that explain why the stars are in their random pattern in the sky, to the stories about the gods that explain thunder and lightning—their anger—or summertime—their pleasure.

In trying to redefine love, I find that almost everyone I know has developed a personal explanation that makes them feel more in control or at least more able to understand the blast of this primal force. My cousin Eliza mentions that a friend has explained to her that in every relationship someone is the cat and someone is the dog. The cat, in Kipling's words in the *Just So* stories, walks by herself. Cats are independent and need no one. She is accustomed to being the cat. Now she is with a man who is a cat; she finds being the dog hard. The dog is the needy one, the one panting for affection, man's best friend. My friend Michael used to say that when they fight, every couple is fighting over who gets to be the child in the relationship. Denis De Rougemont has his theory about the excitement of adversity, Erich Fromm has his ideas about the corrosiveness of our culture, and Helen Fisher has her anthropological necessities.

Some of these theories have been codified and written down in books, and some are still very personal ways of dealing with the soft explosions we all experience in our lives through the medium of our feelings for other people. One morning as we chat about biography, the writer Jon Anderson shares a theory with me. He believes that love has three stages. In the first stage there is discovery: two people finding out that they are alike. In this stage there is an eerie feeling of destiny. Circumstances that don't fit are ignored. The two lovers are amazed that they have found each other—two halves of the same soul, the pot and the lid, the long-lost star-crossed twins. They seem to speak the same language and to have been raised in the same family. They find a dozen similarities in their lives: they are both rich, they are both ugly and smart, they have both always been the only adult in a family of children, they were both born in Colorado.

We are having breakfast at a diner on First Avenue in Manhattan called the Green Kitchen, which is a hangout for recovering alcoholics. At a nearby table I see a handsome older man in deep conversation with a younger man who seems to be reading from a sheet of paper. Their fried eggs are uneaten as they lean together over the coffee in attitudes that can only be the exchanging of Alcoholics Anonymous's fifth step, in which the recovering alcoholic shares his personal inventory—a list of resentments and explanations prescribed in the book *Alcoholics Anonymous*—with another alcoholic. In the corner a man I know slightly is thirteenth-stepping a pretty young girl.

Jon explains the second stage of his theory in which there is disappointment as the lovers realize that they are not alike at all. Suddenly, it seems that no two people could be more different. A different set of facts from the same two lives tells a different story. One has been married and has three children, while the other has never married. One grew up in California and the other in New York. And although they are both in the throes of the temporary addiction that we call love, one is obsessed with sex and has never been able to settle down because of his preoccupation with women and their bodies, while the other has been able to control her impulses. How can two such different people have been attracted to each other? They begin to fight. They call the whole thing off and then reunite at least once.

In the third stage, according to Jon's theory, the two people begin to sort out how they are alike and how they are different. Instead of becoming one united circle or two separate circles, they become overlapping circles with some things in common and some things not in common. This is mature love, the kind on which people can build a life. It's rational. It allows for two individuals to exist without being an affront to what they share. It's flexible enough to accommodate the complexity of human beings. This is the stage that Helen Fisher labels "attachment" and which, in brain imagery, is associated with large doses of oxytocin.

Although in this theory each stage is described as circles—two together, two apart, and two overlapping—in my experience the three stages are not necessarily related. In my life I have been blown away by the force of the first and second stages, but I have had only a few moments of experiencing the third stage, and those moments have not often been with the men with whom I have experienced stages one and two. It's a mistake to assume a link between the addictive stages of love to the rational mature stage. If we understood love this way, as a three-part process in which the first stage, addictive desire, does not automatically lead to the second or third stages, we might change the way we approach marriage. Instead of couples being rushed to the altar once they have "fallen in love," we would urge them to wait two years to see if their connection will become a kind of connection on which they can build a life. In most states we make couples wait at least a year before we allow them to divorce; we make them wait only a few hours before we let them get married.

Ron Gallen is a financial counselor and addiction and recovery specialist in New York City. We meet at Barney Greengrass, a New York institution on Columbus Avenue where crowded tables and peeling wallpaper coexist with smoked salmon that tastes like butter if butter were a fish. Barney Greengrass has been around so long that S. J. Perelman wrote about it; at mealtimes the little room is always crowded, but on off-hours sometimes there will be a movie star quietly scarfing up Barney's famous eggs and salmon in the back—Matthew Broderick, Kevin Kline, Phoebe Cates.

Ron Gallen has been counseling addicts about money disorders for years—he even wrote a book about it called *The Money Trap*. As he finishes his eggs, Ron says the reason why it is so hard to define addiction and what causes it is that nobody really knows. Although everyone I have interviewed has a theory, they are just theories. We go over the most basic theories: addiction is caused by trauma, by genetics, by the body acting out the past, or by underlying psychological imbalances that are being medicated by the substance or behavior.

When I bring up the simplest distinction though—the difference between addictions with a substance, such as alcoholism, eating disorders, cocaine addiction, and the so-called "psychological" addictions that involve no substance, like gambling and sex addiction, Ron disagrees. He would divide addictions in another basic way, between those whose substance or behavior can be put down permanently—addiction to alcohol, cigarettes, cocaine, gambling—and those whose substance has to be dealt with every day by anyone leading a normal life or whose behavior is sometimes normal—problems around money, food, sexual activity.

Recovery from addiction to a substance which can be completely avoided is quite different than recovery from a substance which is part of anyone's life. As people with eating disorders say, trying to eat abstinently is like trying to take a tiger out of a cage three times a day and then coax him back in until the next time. So even on this basic level, we see addiction differently.

Then we proceed to disagree about the definition of addiction in the first place; Ron's is far more extreme than mine. His theory of what causes addiction is best described as "all of the above." He believes that addiction is a deeply rooted and many-tentacled condition which is always a symptom of an underlying psychological imbalance *and* which has a genetic component *and* which is often a result of posttraumatic stress syndrome *and* which is fed by environmental factors like availability and cultural acceptance *and* which is also a response to internal conflict. Although he calls this model a triangle, it sounds more like an octagon. I ask him if he has ever treated a patient with money disorders who does not also have another addiction. He says no.

As we talk and as he describes the way different addictions pair with and nestle inside each other, I am thrown back on an old theory of my own. Maybe there are two kinds of people: addicts and nonaddicts. Perhaps the substance is beside the point, something chosen because of a variety of factors like availability and acceptability by the culture and a particular brain chemistry. A wealthy housewife might find in compulsive shopping, which won't be seen as a problem for a long time, what a college student finds in binge drinking which, in the college community, will also be seen as normal for a long time. So the high-schooler smokes dope and steals from his parents' liquor cabinet, while the businessman rents videos and hires prostitutes on trips to faraway cities, and the college freshman buys bags of groceries, eats them, and vomits in the communal bathroom. Isn't this all really the same thing?

part three

what can we do about it?

let's change the way
we describe addiction

I met Warren in 1972; we stopped speaking in 1978 when I chose to be with the handsome writer; we went back to being occasional friends in 1981. It wasn't until the spring of 1986 that we began to see a lot more of each other. Warren was often in New York, where he liked to stay at the St. Regis, using his *San Francisco Examiner* expense account. By 1986 my second marriage had come apart. In spite of my love for my daughter, I couldn't seem to stop cheating on my husband, her father. Consciously, I desperately wanted to be faithful.

Again and again, I promised myself that I would be. Then something would go wrong. My mother was diagnosed with cancer two years after my father died of cancer in 1982. Her oncologist asked me out for dinner. He spoke to me honestly about her illness at a time when this was rare. He got me pathology reports before they were due; he assured me that with the right treatment she would survive. I was miserable about my mother's illness; I felt that lightning had struck twice in the same place. Returning to the hospital where my father had been treated made me feel sick with fear. I flashed on my father's gaunt face the day he told me he was thinking of killing himself. I remembered the skeletal way he looked when it was time to bring him home to die. How could I assuage the fear that twisted my insides and kept me up at night?

I calmed myself by calling my mother's doctor. I felt safe when I was with him. The doctor lived in a dreary apartment; he didn't read books. When I was there, the fear seemed to lessen. Of course, I slept with him. One afternoon I had fallen asleep on his bed and I was late to get home to my daughter. My husband was away. It was six and the babysitter had said she had to leave at six. Suddenly, I felt trapped in the room that had made me feel so safe. What was I doing there when my daughter needed me?

Whenever there was a crisis, I found a man to help me take the edge off the feelings of helplessness and pain. When my daughter was in the hospital and a lover of mine came to see if he could help, I went back to my apartment and slept with him. Moving men, doctors, lawyers, book salesmen—any man associated with a threatening change in my life became erotically charged, with predictable results. My brother tells a story about a friend who, after a bitter divorce, moved to a strange city. She was alone in a shabby apartment in a bad neighborhood. She married the locksmith who came to put on new locks.

We categorize addiction by substance; perhaps we are thinking about it in the wrong way. Perhaps it should be characterized by intensity. Instead of saying, "He's an alcoholic" or "She's a sex addict," we might say, "He's a level-five addict" or "She's a level-two addict." Some people do seem to be more addicted than others. Some can get through life with "drinking problems," juggling debt or a few divorces and a little adultery, while others are hospitalized, arrested, or institutionalized before they reach the age of consent.

It often seems that even to the addict the substance has a protean flexibility. Substituting addictions, what Pat Carnes calls bargaining with chaos, is almost inevitable. Denied drugs, an addict may quite quickly become an alcoholic. Denied alcohol many addicts will turn to food or shopping, sex, or gambling. "The more we learn about the brain and its chemistry and neuroplasticity, the more it seems, that at least for the version of science that we are just entering, there is a degree of unity to all addictions, substance or process," author Ernest Kurtz wrote me. "I have long suspected this (as have others), having studied Gamblers Anonymous as a control group when I was studying A.A. way back in the 1970's. . . . The ultimate addiction, of course, is materialism."

Patients who have had bariatric surgery, surgery that reduces the size of the stomach and therefore makes it impossible to eat excess quantities of food, find it physically impossible to continue their eating disorders. They find other substances. "A significant fraction of postbariatric patients acquire new addictions like gambling, smoking, compulsive shopping or alcoholism once they are no longer addicted to eating," Stephen J. Dubner and Steven G. Levitt write in the *New York Times Sunday Magazine*. "In certain cases, some people also learn to outfox the procedure by taking in calories in liquid form (drinking chocolate syrup straight from the can, for instance) or simply drinking and eating at the same time."

It's as if the addict is addicted to a feeling rather than a specific substance that triggers the feeling. "There is a simple economics to it," Dr. Amanda Itzkoff writes. "The patient who undergoes surgery ... does not pay the psychological price that would be required to come to understand why he thwarts himself so. And so the psychological problem, having not received its due sum, returns in a new form."

The brain chemistry studies show addiction lighting up the brain's dopamine pathways regardless of the actual substance or activity. Addicts are not addicted to substances; addicts are addicted to the feelings they get from their substances, and if they are denied a substance and they can get that feeling from another substance, they will.

One of the realities of addiction and recovery in the twenty-first century is that many addictions are interchangeable. If you are addicted to one thing, you are probably addicted to many things. Often it appears that when people proclaim themselves cured of an addiction they have actually just switched their addictive needs to a more socially acceptable or less damaging substance, although these two things do not always coincide. If we can separate our idea of addiction from the particular substance used by the addict at a particular time, the whole problem of addiction will take on a different appearance and require a different kind of solution.

There are moral and ethical considerations for an addict to consider as well as the shifting panorama of what society accepts. Smoking, for instance, was once an acceptable addiction but is now unacceptable. The acceptable level of alcohol consumption has also changed in the last decade. It is less acceptable to be so drunk at a dinner party that one gropes the hostess or falls down in the coatroom. On the other hand, binge drinking in colleges appears to be more acceptable.

In other words, all addictions are not equal. Some are more dangerous than others, some are more damaging than others, and some are more socially acceptable than others. Addictions that require other people as a substance have a special moral charge; a serial seducer implicates another person every time he or she switches partners. Like all addictions, sex addiction has a built-in shelf life, as a pharmacist might say. One "falls in love" reveling in the wonderful feelings of high and low, of needs sublimely met, of soaring and sinking. For a while there is no such thing as "too much" with the object of desire. The world shrinks down to a universe of two.

When the dose wears off, however, the sex addict doesn't need more of the same person, he or she needs a new person. Although it is an addiction seemingly condoned by society, sex addiction can be one of the most morally repulsive addictions. Many addictions primarily cause pain to the addict. Sex addiction causes a huge amount of collateral damage. In fact, collateral damage sometimes seems to be its primary result.

The automatic abandonment built into the sex addict's patterns and the "psychic death" the sex addict inflicts on those he or she leaves behind can be compared to what happens to victims of a serial killer, Maggie Scarf argues in her fascinating essay "The Man Who Disappears." Citing a presentation titled "The Structure of Evil" by Christopher Bollas, Scarf points out that the selection of a vulnerable person (the prey), the seduction of that person, and the betrayal and abandonment of that person is a pattern common to the serial killer and the serial seducer. Both people seem to be in the grip of a compulsion, and in both cases the compulsion damages someone else.

In *Love Sick,* Sue William Silverman compares her own patterns of sex addiction to the patterns of serial killer Jeffrey Dahmer. "In my liquid hot steel nights I must must must endlessly duplicate the familiarity of my dangerous childhood as closely as possible. . . .

A therapist I once saw on television explained Jeffrey Dahmer, the serial killer and cannibal from Milwaukee, in this manner. He is the ultimate mayhem of liquid hot steel nights of addictive rage. In a specific bar he meets a specific kind of man on a specific kind of night who reminds him of his soul's devastation. . . . He devours love. He devours sex. He wants to control and dominate and devour you. . . . Since all addicts are serial," she continues, "the ritual must begin again. The fuck, the murder, the bottle of scotch, the Oreo cookie do not provide everlasting love or solace, so we must try it, hope for it, with the next seductive fuck, murder, drink, piece of cake. Just one more time. Again and again."

Whether or not it is a legitimate comparison—and it seems very extreme to compare a Don Juan or a woman who commits adultery or someone who eats too many cookies to a serial killer—there are certainly severe moral questions about the effects of sex addiction.

Like all addicts, someone who is addicted to sex can morph into someone with an eating disorder, someone with an alcohol problem, or even—as is commonly mentioned—someone who is "addicted" to twelve-step programs. The difference between a serial killer and a man or woman who has been married twice and is again cheating on their spouse can be understood not as a difference in kind—both may be addicts—but as a difference in degree, in the intensity of their need for the feelings provided by their substance and by their behavior. This difference sometimes seems to depend on the level of the childhood trauma inflicted on the addict, but not always.

Sometime in 1986, Warren and I began to meet for dinner with his daughter in New York. She had been a toddler when we fell in love; she had grown into a beautiful, talented woman. The three of us had a wonderful time together; we shared a black sense of humor and a taste for expensive Italian food. When Warren went back to San Francisco, she and I had lunch together. She told me that her father had kept her up all night explaining that he loved me and that he had always loved me. She said she thought it was very sad that we were not together.

That Easter the three of us took my four-year-old daughter up to my mother's house in Westchester for Easter dinner. It was odd being back in the house where Warren had first come to visit with his wife, and where he and my father had first decided they didn't like each other. Now my father was dead and Warren was alone. My mother welcomed him at dinner and he poured her an Irish whiskey. She had always liked Warren. Although my mother had stayed for four decades with a man she didn't seem to like, she was always on the side of true love. That night, after his daughter had gone home and my daughter was asleep, Warren told me he thought we should be together again. We would get married, he said, and have the child we never got to have.

a community of one

The one thing shared by most addicts, no matter what the substance, is a feeling of alienation. This happens for a number of reasons. One is that the addict—especially if he or she has been traumatized—feels that they see the world as it really is while everyone else exists in a fool's paradise. Patrick Carnes calls this the addict's belief system, the delusional mind of the addict. But this conviction that one sees clearly while everyone else is in a Pollyanna fog is more than a belief, it is as deep as the marrow in our bones. The human balance that enables most people to live without mind-altering substances every day is fragile. It can be upset by trauma or by witnessing trauma. Once you see what people can do to each other, it's hard to go back to the level of trust in strangers and the human community that makes life bearable.

And sex is such an appealing substance. We live in a culture that promotes sex constantly. Our understanding is that everyone has a right to good sex. If they have sexual dysfunction, they can take a drug. If they are clumsy, they can rent an instructional video. Celibacy is actually frowned on in our society. Few have read G. K. Chesterton's brilliant essay on the excitements of celibacy, which, he argues, is not an absence of sex (any more than white is the absence of color) but a state of being in itself. Monks with their sacred vows of celibacy, poverty, and obedience are archaic old men. Why would anyone want to be any of those things? If people don't have partners, they are suspect. If they don't have sex with their partners, there is something wrong with them. Sex at first seems as innocent as alcohol. Who doesn't want sex and as much of it as they can possibly get?

In all addictions there is a rupturing of the individual's connection to society—a breaking of the social contract, the divorce of a single man or woman from the human race. Like the melting of the arctic ice, this alienation has a momentum of its own. A sex addict has to keep secrets. If he or she is married, all sexual activity outside the marriage is probably secret. Secrets are delicious. They make you feel special and powerful. You, the secret holder, know what's really going on while the rest of the world troops along in ignorance. Secrets divide people. I have a friend who told his wife he wouldn't mind if she was unfaithful as long as she didn't hide it from him. "It's not the sex that destroys a marriage," he would say. "It's the secret."

For people who have grown up in families with secrets or in addicted families, secrets seem to hold the power to survive. Of course, secrets are a powerful means of isolation. If you have secrets, you can't relax. You move through the world carrying a ticking time bomb. If anyone knew what you were really thinking, the whole world would come crashing down on you.

What makes us human? What energy source enables us to get up every day and make that first cup of tea or coffee? What makes us resilient enough to bounce back after the end of a job or a relationship, strong and flexible enough for the impossible job of raising children, loving enough to have friends?

We measure our status by the community we inhabit: What parties do we get invited to? Who wants to publish our work or use our professional skills? When our status soars, our community rejoices for us and with us. When our status sinks, it is our community that we fall back on. They love us anyway. They understand. This community is usually made up of friends, family, and colleagues. It shifts as our children grow. For a while I had a lovely community with other parents at my son's school. After we dropped off the kids in the morning, we all had coffee. When we picked them up in the afternoon, we all hung out in the schoolyard. The kids grew up and started going to school on their own, and that community shifted.

Community is usually centered on people we know well and see frequently, but it also extends to people we don't know personally—our government representatives, the writers and broadcasters to whom we listen regularly and whom we consider wise, our "buddies" on the television programs we watch each week. "Every community is an association of some kind and every community is established with a view to some good, for everyone always acts in order to obtain that which they think good," wrote Aristotle. "But, if all communities aim at some good, the state or political community, which is the highest of all, and which embraces all the rest, aims at good in a greater degree than any other, and at the highest good." As human beings, our first need is for community.

One sign of an emerging addiction is a shift in community. "At first Anna had avoided this society of Princess Tverskoy's as much as she could," writes Tolstoy of the world, "but after her visit to Moscow it turned the other way around. She avoided her virtuous friends and went out into the great world. There she met Vronsky and experienced an exciting joy at these meetings."

The Internet explosion of community is evidence of how much we crave people like ourselves, people who will listen to us and understand us and share their own experience with us. MySpace, YouTube, and Facebook are all ways of extending our communities from personal to those outside our daily rounds. This craving for connection with other people, people like us, people who speak our language and can understand our experience because they have had the same kinds of experiences, is the most fundamental human desire.

A couple is a community of two. Whether it is a couple in love or a couple having sex in a motel bedroom, their community collapses. There are only two people in the world. Slowly, that community enlarges. Soon enough we become impatient to introduce our loved one to our friends. If we have children we love, we want them to love our children too. We want to share them and we want them to share. Many relationships that might have thrived if they took place on a desert island have been shipwrecked on the rocks of community. Other relationships, anemic at best when left alone, begin to thrive in a shared community.

One of the reasons we make such a fuss about marriage is that it signifies the rejoining of this community of two with the larger community. We invite our community to our weddings and announce that we are promising them that we will be good husbands and wives legally and physically and emotionally—a much stronger promise than the promises we make in quiet rooms or lying back on a pillow after lovemaking. Private promises are subject to misinterpretation and to being forgotten. *You said I could be free and that you wanted me to feel our love encompassed the whole world. That didn't mean I gave you permission to sleep with my brother.*

Public promises, especially accompanied by ministers and parents, are harder to forget and even harder to misinterpret. So although being in love starts out with a drastic curtailment of community, it ends with a reassertion of the importance of a larger community.

An addict is a community of one. Addiction, particularly addiction to other people, often starts before the addict becomes a slave to the substance. It starts with isolation, a division between the person and the community. Often, people who become sex addicts or who are addicted to love have been molested as children, but there are many, many ways to fall into the sense of alienation and anxious apartness that is the fertile field for addiction.

A child can watch another family member get molested and, charged with keeping this dreadful secret, feel completely separated from everyone else on earth. "The terminal point of addiction is what is called damnation," the poet W.H. Auden wrote.

This is why twelve-step programs are a great force against addiction. Addiction is hugely forceful. It provides comfort, a feeling of belonging and a feeling of power in a world where the addict has often felt powerless. But it separates the addict from the rest of society in a way that is profoundly damaging, in a way that causes a despair that feeds the addiction.

A twelve-step program creates a community of addicts. An addict walking into a meeting finds others with the same secrets and others with the same problems. This community, instead of being shocked when it hears the addict tell his or her secrets, laughs or nods in agreement and reaches out in love. Addicts often say that when they walk into their first twelve-step meeting they feel at home for the first time. No wonder. This is an alternate community, a community that heals the addict by replacing the old community from which he or she had been torn by circumstance and by volition. That's what we all need to move through life, a sense of community.

In Yale surgeon Sherwin Nuland's best-selling book *The Art of Aging,* he stresses the power of community for people who want to age gracefully, people whose attitudes help them be loving, substantial members of society as they slide into their seventies and eighties. He quotes Yale professor Leo Cooney, an expert on aging who founded the section on geriatrics at Yale Medical School, as saying that although exercise is important for those who would age well, it is not more important than community. "Exercise is not the Holy Grail," Cooney tells Nuland. "If there's a Holy Grail it's relationships with other people. In fact, if you have to decide between going to the gym or being with your grandchildren, I'd choose your grandchildren."

For an infant, connections to other people are necessary to survive. For an adult, connections to others are the key to a sane and happy life. It is these connections that are compromised and finally killed off by addiction. An addict replaces other people with the substance even when, as in sex and love addiction, the substance *is* other people. As connections to other people that involve give-and-take and responsibilities to loved ones take a back seat, the addict begins the hungry search for something else embodied in other people, strangers, people who are not part of the community but rather draw him away from the community. Community heals us; addiction destroys us.

"Only connect! That was the whole of her sermon," says E. M. Forster's Margaret Schlegel in his novel *Howard's End.* "Only connect the prose and the passion, and both will be exalted, and human love will be seen at its height. Live in fragments no longer. Only connect, and the beast and the monk, robbed of the isolation that is life to either, will die." These two words, "Only connect," are perhaps Forster's most famous. This yearning for connection is at the heart of the human condition. Community is the ultimate form of connection, a place in which individuals brought together because of family ties, or ideological ties, or both, support and protect each other.

The dailyness of our lives is fueled by community and our faith in community. I get up in the morning to get my son off to school, a school where he is loved and has his own community. Then I'm off to meet with a few friends for an early-morning walk. And it's my sense of being a member of a community that is at the heart of my creative energy. Audience is a kind of community. Without the faith in community that enables me to think that something I write will make a difference to someone out there—a reader—I wouldn't be able to write. What would be the point?

I often say that writing is a dialogue in the form of a monologue. The best writing is collaboration between writer and reader, between a writer and his or her community. As the late Allen Ginsberg wrote: "Fortunately art is a community effort—a small but select community living in a spiritualized world endeavoring to interpret the wars and the solitudes of the flesh."

storytelling

The British psychologist Sir Frederic Bartlett, who studied memory, has used the term "effort at meaning" to describe the way we turn our past histories into stories that suit our psychological patterns. Joan Didion has said that we tell ourselves stories in order to live. So when we look back at our lives, like writers, we pick out the details that tell the story we are hard-wired to tell. I can look back at my own history and see it as a life of great adventure and passion, or I can look back and see it as a life of trauma and addiction. I have the ability to choose how I tell my story to myself and others. Still, I know that usually when something is either/or, the actuality is that it's both.

This urge, the urge to tell stories about ourselves that explain our past and project our futures, is why so many people want to be writers. Having a voice in the world is one of the strongest human urges. "All I have is a voice to undo the folded lie," W. H. Auden wrote. That's one of the things that makes being a writer seem desirable.

It's also the fact that, whether or not we ever sit down at a keyboard or take pen in hand, we are all storytellers working on the story of our own experience. Every one of us takes the meaningless cloth, the yards and yards of life experience that flows over us and through us each day and the millions and millions of things that happen to each of us in an hour, and shapes it and reshapes it and reshapes it again until it makes sense to us. This is storytelling at its most primitive and often at its most powerful. All understanding of the human condition, from Homer to Freud to Oprah to my discussion with my son at dinnertime tonight, depends on this desire that we have to understand our lives in terms of stories and this ability that we have to fashion the stories that will give our lives some sense in the context of the previous stories we have told ourselves.

Details are the way we communicate. Each choice of detail—and every utterance or written sentence requires choices—is one of the building blocks of storytelling. I can say that I met a man who is tall, dark, and handsome, or I can say that I met a man who was lanky, swarthy, and had a huckster's smile and describe the same man. I can write that as the child of a respected and adventurous writer I was taken to Rome, where I played in the Roman Forum, and that I took tennis lessons on Nantucket and summered in New Hampshire, or I can say that my parents were miserable partly because my father was a closeted gay alcoholic and that he sometimes took it out on me. Both are true. Even two or three details added together tell a story. The way we choose details and then the way we combine them has absolute control over the way we see our history and the way we see ourselves.

This is one of the things that make addiction so baffling and frustrating; in terms of a conventional narrative, it doesn't make sense. When it comes to that moment of temptation no matter what we understand, we pick up that glass of wine or that telephone or we walk into that hotel room. Many addicts are very intelligent by real-world standards. They do well on their SATs and go to Ivy League schools. They can crunch numbers and do amazing things with computers. But when it comes to their substance, they get stupid. Alcoholics call alcohol "stupid soup." No matter how high a person's IQ or how extensive their knowledge of the Roman Empire or the lives of a cell, when faced with their substance, they do the dumbest thing they could possibly do—they use. The powerlessness of insight, the uselessness of understanding, is one of the things that make recovery from addiction so difficult. Most of us go through life seeking understanding and then acting on the basis of that understanding. This works for most problems, but it does not work for addiction.

One of the first steps in recovery from any addiction is a shift in the way the addict tells the story of his or her life. As long as an addict sees herself as a femme fatale, a woman always surrounded by men, someone who knows how to flirt, a popular queen bee with two or three marriages behind her, she is unlikely to imagine that she is a sex addict. If sexuality is part of her identity, her addiction will be hidden. If a man imagines himself as a Don Juan, a charming, sexy guy who loves the ladies, he is unlikely to have any sense that any of that is a problem.

It's the shift in the stories we tell ourselves about ourselves that makes change possible. Sometimes the memory has to pry the story away from its teller for a few awful seconds so that the pretty woman suddenly flashes on a seedy hotel room where she spent an afternoon with the family doctor while her daughter waited to be picked up from school. Sometimes the memory seems to shift on its own. Sometimes environmental pressures—other people's opinions, another doctor's warning, the way the daughter looks after waiting an hour for an absent mother—can effect a shift. Nothing changes until the story changes.

When we tell our daughters that a man will complete them, when we read them "Cinderella," or when we lean on our sons to give us grandchildren, we are trying to shape the stories they tell themselves. We tell ourselves that we need to get married because everyone does, ignoring the fact that marriage itself is a protean, shape-changing institution that was invented by each community to serve itself.

Warlike societies promote early marriages and easy divorces because this provides more sons for them to send to the battlefront. Societies based on property ownership have marriage laws and traditions that protect property through relaxed rules about inbreeding and divorce laws that make the dissolution of a marriage next to impossible. Some cultures express their disdain for women, especially women beyond childbearing years, through their marriage laws. Others express their respect for the older women of their community. Although marriage itself is not constant, our longing for it seems to be constant. In all communities it seems to have become a symbol of connection.

My sexual history began in fits and starts, groping and guilt, in my freshman year of college. By then I knew, as only the ignorant can know, that my primary job in life was to land the right man. My parents had repeatedly told me that finding a husband was my goal, and that with my round face and tendency to talk back I probably wouldn't find one. This imagined husband would be handsome and smart and probably rich. He would impress my parents. He would not embarrass me. Like the perfect dress, he would enhance the social self that to me seemed unacceptable, although I had already learned to pretend to great confidence. I watched carefully to see which girls succeeded. By junior year some were already sporting diamond rings, and we all knew that this meant they were sleeping with their boyfriends.

The first man I brought home to my parents was a slender guy who had created a literary identity for himself out of a tweed jacket, horn-rimmed glasses, and a few memorized Yeats poems. He was actually the son of a shop supervisor at Ford's River Rouge plant outside Detroit. We were a couple of fakes, made for each other, playing the pretty literary heiress and her erudite boyfriend, although we both knew that this act was only skin-deep. Our relationship was all about literary drama. He would ask why we couldn't sleep together; I would put the back of my hand to my forehead and quote Yeats. "Others because you did not keep / That deep-sworn vow have been friends of mine," I would intone while he fiddled with his glasses and looked romantically into the distance where the factories of East Providence belched and billowed.

It was evening when we arrived at the house where my family had lived for two years, although we all pretended that we had always lived there. "It must have been wonderful to grow up here," my boyfriend said, looking longingly at the shelves of books flanking the apple-wood fire in the library and the lawns sloping down to a meandering stream. "Mmmm," I said, not quite lying. I had grown up in a different house, a dark room in a remodeled tool shed, which we rented at the whim and pleasure of a wealthy family who liked to think they were patronizing the arts in general and who were fond of my father in particular.

Now at last my parents had moved into the place that looked like what we had always thought we should have. I had the boyfriend who looked the part. There was some fumbling. My father thought that he was obligated to take the boyfriend out in the woods with the chain saw or the shotgun, both of which entirely baffled my father; he was a small man with no mechanical ability who had grown up as the son of a small-town businessman who was ruined by the Depression. In pretending to be a masculine paterfamilias, he was playing a part for which he was eminently unqualified.

As a ritual, my father would heft the small chain saw, fill the tiny engine with gasoline, rev up the motor, and hold the saw while it dug into a log—preferably a soft log conveniently placed. My father's public image was manufactured, which anyone could have discerned. He posed for photos on riding horses from the local stable; horses that hadn't cantered in years. He was usually surrounded by hunting dogs, but these dogs had never seen a bird or a gun and they slept on the couches in the living room. The purpose of all this was to distract visitors from his secrets. His saving grace was that even as he pretended to be something he was not, he made fun of himself for pretending. We all followed suit. He tried desperately to get me to play a good game of tennis, sit a horse well, sail a boat, and ski like a pro, with very mixed results—all of this despite the fact that he did not excel at these things himself.

These staged antics would seem sillier except they fooled almost everyone. My father is still referred to as a dapper, Republican country squire by writers who should know better. People ask me what it was like to have a tall, well-dressed man as my father, or they assume that I have inherited a trust fund as well as the ability to sit a horse and sail a boat.

My father and the boyfriend might have had a few things in

common—both were completely self-invented—but of course neither of them could admit those things. They had to pretend that an aristocratic jaunt in the autumn woods was their birthright. Even when it came to sex, the whole thing was a sham. My parents' marriage was a real connection and a perfect hiding place.

Once, in the precious years after he was sober, my father became convinced that a reporter had guessed that he was gay. It wouldn't have been hard to guess. He traveled with a handsome "protégé," his work is suffused with longing for men, and his closest friends were often gay. This particular reporter had not guessed my father's secret, and in fact during my father's lifetime no reporter guessed his secret. I did not guess his secret.

My father asked me to talk to this reporter, a delicate conversation since I did not know that my father was gay and neither did the reporter. I was supposed to head off this guy's conclusions, conclusions that even I hadn't drawn. Always eager to help, I called the reporter, and we had one of the most uncomfortable conversations I can remember.

The addict has to create a Potemkin self, a surface for the world which cannot guess that he is drunk or high or that he had sex with the gardener before he came down to breakfast. Addiction grows in the dark places created by secrets. There are many causes, of course: there is brain chemistry and genetic predisposition, and there is character and opportunity. Most of all, there are secrets and fakery, worlds created to mask the real world and images meant to fool everyone. Addicts are brilliant storytellers, and my father was one of the best.

In New York City where I live, it is fashionable for women to complain that there are no available men, and as the slaves to fashion that they are, they do complain. I've noticed that what they mean is that there are no available men with handsome faces and lean bodies within the age range of one to five years older than they are with an income significantly larger than their own. There are certainly plenty of men in New York. I've also noticed that many of these women are far happier, more serene, doing better work, having more fun raising their children single than they were when they were married. For every woman who complains that there are no men, there are two women who complain about the man they have. The contentment of the single woman in our society is one of our best-kept secrets.

We are so infatuated with love that the heart shape has replaced the circle. Valentine's Day is as big as Easter. Advertisements almost always show couples, happy couples, happy couples doing happy-couple things. Huge billboards broadcast the ecstasy of two people touching each other. Television dramas pair people off as if the writers were all playing Go Fish with their characters.

When I was a young girl, I knew in my bones (I was told many times but it was also in the air) that I would get married, that getting married was my ultimate destiny. That was the story I told myself. I was twenty-three when I got my first proposal. That was how women talked in those days. They measured their worth on a basis of how many proposals they had received before finally succumbing to the lucky man who was their husband. Mine wasn't even a real proposal with a purchased ring, but it was as close as I had come, and I privately thought as close as I was likely to come.

I was teaching in a small town in Colorado near Aspen, and a man I had been seeing over the summer asked me to come home at Christmas and stay. He wanted me to quit my job for him! That, I thought, was love. He wrote me a letter saying that he didn't want to spend Christmas driving over icy roads and knowing that I would be going back to Colorado. He wanted me to come to New York and live with him. Although he didn't actually ask me to marry him until a few weeks after Christmas, we both knew what he meant.

At that point my longing for connection completely took over my ability to make a sane decision. My friends and my father told me not to go. They pointed out that I had a job I loved and friends I loved. "Marriage brings one into fatal connection with custom and tradition, and traditions and customs are like the wind and weather, altogether incalculable," wrote Kierkegaard.

But the voice I heard in the dark heart of my being was the voice of an older, married woman I taught with.

"You should go," she said. "If you don't, he might not wait for you." This was the voice of fear. This was the view that the world is teeming with women scheming and able to take away those who love us.

The voice of reason might have pointed out that if a man loved me enough to build a life with me he might be able to wait six months in order to possess me. The voice of reason might have said that if a man couldn't wait six months to marry me, he might not be the kind of person with whom I should think about having and raising children and sharing an entire life. The voice of reason was on vacation. I couldn't go back to New York fast enough. I left Colorado before Christmas, bought a wedding dress in February, and was married by the beginning of May. I married a man as panicked as I was, a man who seemed to think I would disappear if he let me out of his sight for too long. I was eager to be swallowed up by love and marriage. My stationery, ordered from Cartier along with invitations, bore my new married name. I was thrilled.

how others tell the story

"The culture is deeply invested in not recognizing that we have a problem," Michael Ryan wrote me, "and I'm sure you are already aware of the general resistance to the idea of sex addiction despite the fact that its consequences surface in the headlines so often." The way we tell ourselves the stories of who we are and how we live may purposefully delete the possibility of addiction, but we live in a culture that does the same thing. We both ignore addiction and indulge in a fascination with it at a safe distance.

Every day there are stories about sex and love addiction in the newspaper, but they are rarely reported that way. Whether it's a man who murders a woman who rejects him, or a president who jeopardizes the highest office in the world for a sexy intern, or a congressman sending mash notes to a page, or a mayor who announces that he's leaving his wife at a press conference, or a governor forced to resign in a call-girl scandal, there is plenty of coverage of the story of sexual acting out, and little mention of addiction. In stories like this, stories in which the action is caused by someone's compulsion to be self-destructive or someone's sexual obsession, there are always many personal details, but rarely any mention of the underlying problem.

Valentine's Day is two days away, and the *New York Times* announced in yesterday's Ideas and Trends section that "the love drug" is a powerful one. As an example, it uses the story of Lisa Nowak, an astronaut who was arrested when she drove cross country in a diaper with a BB gun and some rubber hose to confront Colleen Shipman, a rival for the affections of a man. The story quotes Arthur Aron, a SUNY-Stonybrook professor who has been on television a lot: "[Love] trumps the desire for wealth, for power, even to live." It quotes Helen Fisher and her experiment showing that MRI scans of rejected lovers show decreased blood flow to the decision-making area of the brain and increased activity in the dopamine reward system, creating what Fisher calls "abandonment rage." "You've got a person who has enormous energy and intense motivation and craving with focused attention, willing to take huge risks, in physical pain, trying to control their anger, and obsessively thinking about someone," Fisher said. "It's a bad combination."

When we say that drugs in general and the love drug in particular make people do crazy things, we restrict ourselves to the kind of craziness that is a little bit funny. Oh, those crazy people! The nutty astronaut, the runaway bride, the vengeful ex-girlfriend who unplugs the water bed. The scissored-off pant legs, the slashed evening clothes. We love to read about Jean Harris, who shot her philandering lover. She was such a lady; the contrast between the perfect WASP headmistress and the crazy, murdering rejected woman holds us in its thrall. We like to read about Clara Harris, who ran over her cheating husband with her Mercedes, and Burt Pugach, who hired thugs to throw lye in the face of the woman he was dating—who later married him.

When we do admit that love is sometimes just like a drug and not a coming together of two souls in preparation for building a life together, we have to mitigate our description. We have to make a joke of it. It's a yuk-yuk kind of thing, the way we describe the love drug. Are we covering up our fear of these deep, irresistible forces? We don't laugh at alcoholics having delirium tremens; we turn away in disgust. We don't laugh when a heroin addict is in withdrawal; we call 911 for an ambulance. When someone is in withdrawal from sex addiction though, with all the pain and agony and craziness we should know that engenders, we somehow find it funny.

Few people like to call themselves addicts. One of the mainstays of describing addiction without using the A-word is William James's *Varieties of Religious Experience*. The book is a series of lectures, the Gifford Lectures, which James gave in Edinburgh in 1901–2. In one of the most often-quoted lectures, Lecture Eight, "The Divided Self, and the Process of Its Unification," James proposes that there are two kinds of people. The first type is what he calls the once-born. These are men and women with lives whose satisfaction can be measured by weighing the good against the bad.

The second type of person in James's dialectic is the twice-born, or what he quotes Alphonse Daudet as calling "homo duplex." The life of the twice-born can't be measured in the usual way, because that life is complicated and contains darkness as well as light. Using St. Augustine as an example, James tells the story of the change in the Carthaginian saint who, "distracted by the struggle between the two souls in his breast, and ashamed of his own weakness of will, heard a voice which told him to pick up the Bible where, opening at random, he saw an invocation against wantonness," which, as James writes, "laid the inner storm to rest forever."

This famous description of the divided self often sounds like the addicted self. James describes the conflict between the self that knows what ought to be done and the same self acknowledging its inability to do it. As St. Paul wrote: "The good I would, I do not, and that I would not, that I do, O wretched man that I am."

Any addict reading these words or picking through James's rich and dense prose feels a shock of recognition and relief. His or her condition is not a new thing. It's not just the stuff of rehabs and memoirs and twelve-step meetings; addiction as St. Paul and James describe it is part of the human condition for many men and women and it always has been.

My father, in the seven years of his sobriety, was a changed man. He went from being an invalid who sat in the yellow wing chair sniping at anything he happened to notice, to being a loving man engaged with the universe. He went from being furious if dinner was not served on time to learning how to cook and serve dinner himself. It was as if he had just awakened from a long sleep. He wanted to learn how things worked. He wanted to learn to run the dishwasher.

It was easy to see that my father was an alcoholic. He had a bad bout of delirium tremens in the hospital during which he thought he was flying a plane and then that the food carts were Russian ammunition trucks. He fell down and spilled things and got Driving While Under the Influence tickets—Dooeys, we called them for D.U.I.'s. He was also a chain-smoker, and this too stopped miraculously a few years after he got sober.

His addictive connection to sex was never addressed. His work and his conversation always had a quality of romantic yearning that he certainly passed on to us children and, to some extent, to his readers. It's the longing voice, the sad longing voice interspersed with hope that makes the stories so powerful. For decades my father had been falling in and out of love with other men. His affair with Calvin Kentfield in Hollywood when he was there writing screenplays was so intense and frightened my father so badly that he refused to go back to Los Angeles even though he might have been able to make more money there than he could at home. His journals around this time bristle with confusion.

Almost every time I run into the composer Ned Rorem, he tells me about having my father over to his apartment for a drink. There they were, two literary men and some sherry, until Ned's partner Jim Holmes came home. According to Ned, my father was electrified and began wooing Holmes, who backed away. A small chase around the apartment resulted in my father being rejected. The startling thing about this story is what I know that Ned doesn't. My father caught the 6:20 train home to Scarborough later that evening in time to preside at the family dinner table over a meal cooked by my mother. What was he thinking as he scolded me for wanting second helpings of mashed potatoes? In my deep well of self-hatred there was no chance that I would notice the emotional lipstick on his collar. My mother, the same.

At my brother Ben's writer's group lunch I talk with the writer Larkin Warren, who was one of the writers of the book *Addiction: Why Can't They Just Stop?* which was written to go with the HBO special series on addiction. Larkin is very sure about the nature of addiction: she says it is genetic. Brain scans and genetic tests show that even when people who have the physical hallmarks of addiction don't drink or use drugs or act out, the propensity is still there lying latent in their genes.

Over scallop salad we all talk about the ways addiction works.

We are supposed to be talking about writing, but when the subject of addiction comes up, it seems to suck all the air out of the dialogue. Because there is still a mystery at the heart of addiction, especially addiction to sex and love, it seems to take over almost every conversation. The mystery goes beyond genetics, environment, and trauma. No one knows whether rehabs really help or if they work better with alcoholism than with sex addiction, for instance. There have been no ten-year studies of people in twelve-step programs. In addiction there is no Framingham study—a fifty-year study of 5,000 men and women from Framingham, Massachusetts, and their children and grandchildren—conducted by Boston University and the National Heart Institute—which has yielded valuable information about heart disease, genetics, and many other medical conditions.

Helen Fisher thinks that twelve-step programs succeed because they have the benefits of the hunting and gathering society of our ancestors. Everyone is equal, and there is a kind of God in the book *Alcoholics Anonymous.* The culture of recovery is nomadic because everywhere you go there are meetings, and it also depends on a local community. When I ask about her voluminous citations of psychological studies, she tells me that she has recently cleaned out a lot of boxes filled with studies that were out of date. "The last time I broke up with a man, I was so angry that I had the energy to do all this cleaning," she says. "It's okay, he's back, but the whole front of my closet got cleaned out."

conscience and remorse

Alcoholics in Alcoholics Anonymous say that if you take the alcohol away from the alcoholic you are left with the "ic." One of the puzzles of addiction is its latency behavior—it's a sleeping horror. An addict is an addict even without his or her substance. Stories and studies show that addicts who have no way to use and no substance available can go for years or even decades without igniting their addiction. Then there comes a time—alone in a hotel room, at a party, or just late on a boring Sunday afternoon—when a switch seems to be turned on. The substance is in front of them, and the dreadful cycle begins as if it had been waiting there all along.

Charles Darwin believed that the human conscience was the principal thing that delineated humans from animals. What is the connection of conscience to addiction? Shouldn't the one preclude the other? Conscience also seems to be the one thing that delineates normal people from addicts. How did we develop a conscience?

One anthropologist, Michael Chance, reasoned that it came about as a way to get ahead in the world. Chance reasoned that in order to influence the older, more powerful males in a pack and to work their way up, young males had to "equilibrate"—to balance alternatives and control their sexual and aggressive drives. Those who could act from the head rather than the heart were the ones who survived.

Anthropologist Robin Fox has pointed out that, as social life emerged, young men had to follow stringent rules about whom they could court and whom they must avoid. Women, of course, had to follow equally intricate and even more stringent rules. This system led to guilt, to a feeling almost always of having broken the rules when it comes to sex. Guilty people begin to conceal their behavior whether or not it merits concealment. They learn to lie. They become separated from those around them. They lose their human connection and their community. In a classic flip into addiction, their power begins to come from bad behavior—from secrets—rather than from good behavior.

Fox theorizes that the seat of the conscience is in the amygdala, while other scientists think that when we obey the rules the brain releases endorphins and the dopamine pathways light up—doing good feels good. In an addict these normal stimulus responses seem to have been wired in backward. The addict gets high from breaking the rules even when there is no substance or person involved. A normal person can find a source of pleasure in appropriate sexual abstinence by not sleeping with a fiancé before marriage, for instance, or by not sleeping with someone else's husband or a wife's sister or other forbidden individuals. An addict finds pleasure in quietly breaking the rules and temporarily fooling everyone.

My cousin Frank Griswold invites me for dinner at his daughter's apartment downtown in Battery Park. Frank and I come from different branches of the same family. His grandmother, a sharp-witted New Haven society woman named Polly Whitney, married my grandfather, the feisty dean of the Yale Medical School. Both brought children to the marriage, children who are still reeling from the collision. It's a family with some blessings and some curses: fierce intelligence, wit, a tradition of service, alcoholism.

I have known Frank for years; when I was an awkward teen, he and his brother swept into our family summer place and whisked me away, telling my parents they were taking me to see a movie called *The Secret Life of Walter Mitty*. Instead they took me to see *A Place in the Sun*, which had been released a few years earlier and finally made it to a small town in New Hampshire. With Montgomery Clift and Elizabeth Taylor, and based on a Theodore Dreiser novel, the movie radiated sexual heat with every frame. I sat there transfixed as I watched what can happen when a man and a woman are swept away by the force of sexual desire. Did I want to be the overweight, unwanted Shelley Winters as Alice—called "Al"—who seems stupid and slow-moving even as she allows herself to get pregnant and then get murdered? Or did I want to be the dazzling Elizabeth Taylor with her enchanting laugh and careless attitude about other people's feelings. No contest.

There is something comforting about Frank. He's funny and literate and he seems to have dodged most of our family's bad mojo. From January 1998 until November 2006, Frank was the presiding bishop of the Episcopal Church, and I am thrilled that I will have a chance to chat with him about sex addiction. He has great natural authority and talks about faith and about God in ways that are direct and persuasive.

Frank puts our dinner in the oven and I start by asking him

about remorse. Nonaddicts make mistakes and do stupid things, but they move on. The addict feels remorse so sharp that it often requires medication from the drug or activity that caused the problem in the first place. Remorse is one of the linchpins of the addictive cycle.

Frank points out that in Christianity remorse is a good thing. St. Augustine says that remorse is God's voice, the moment when the addict comes to, and realizes the error of his ways. Remorse is the epiphany that breaks the cycle. Frank and I have some fun acting out the alcoholic remorse that was so much a part of both of our childhoods: the sobbing, the apologies, the slurred words as each of our fathers promised again and again that they would stop drinking, that whatever happened would never happen again.

It's easy to make fun of, but of course the addict really believes these promises, promises that will soon be broken. In the Wilson family Bible there is a whole page of Bill Wilson's promises to Lois that he will never drink again. He meant it; he meant it! He staked his new business on never drinking again, signed a contract saying he would never drink again, obviously really believed that the negative consequences of drinking were so great that he would indeed never drink again. Addicts always know that they must not do it. Montgomery Clift had been warned again and again about dating workers in the Eastman factory, much less getting them pregnant. But he did it anyway. In fact, it was remorse and the futility of remorse that eventually led Bill Wilson to acknowledge his absolute powerlessness. That admission is what some people believe is the first step toward recovery.

Addiction subverts the conscience of the addict. Instead of having the normal human reaction of pleasure in sharing a sense of the rules that order the social contract, the addict gets pleasure from breaking the social contract. Even if he or she doesn't murder anyone (and usually they don't), the addict is always an outlaw, looking in from the lonely places where addiction isolates its victims. This is one of the things that make healing addiction so difficult. Addicts can't really hear "normal" people counsel them, and many normal people still stigmatize addicts as people with not enough willpower. It takes an addict to reach an addict.

As a young woman in college, I learned about addictive behavior patterns almost as soon as I started dating. After a few disasters, contemptuous men, and long crying jags in the dorm at night that left me feeling puffy and unlovable, I slowly came to understand how the game was played. I learned that people want what they can't have; that what we call love can only grow in a vacuum. I found out that the less a man knew me the more he would pursue me, that in fact the way the world works was the opposite of what I had heard. I would be the dazzling careless Angela instead of the plodding, loyal Alice.

Later, I developed what I now call the Jack Higgins rule, a cruel way to separate those who are addicted from those who are not. Jack was a lawyer and a successful hedge fund manager who had a series of beautiful women as girlfriends, but none of them lasted. He was rich and powerful and they were just chasing his money, he said; or if they weren't chasing his money, they collapsed on him and took all the oxygen out of the relationship. I advised him to court a woman heavily and then withdraw for two weeks. After two weeks he should call. If the woman scolded him, she wasn't for him. If the woman was friendly and caring, if the woman made it clear that his presence in her life—although delightful—was not that important, then she was a real one. This kind of insouciance, this negation of normal feelings is also heavily promoted in many dating books. It works well; both men and women are at-tracted to other men and women who take everything lightly. It is also dangerous. It is not a good way to find a partner.

Years later I ran into Jack himself at a dinner party. It was the best kind of New York City party, with powerful men and beautiful women packed into a book-lined space. There were flowers every-where, and as I scanned the room, there were little shocks of recog-nition and pleasure as I recognized famous people and as I picked out the faces of old friends, people I hadn't seen in a long time, people I loved to talk with. Jack was standing with his back to the bar and it was a crowded room, so we had one of those conversa-tions in which half of what is said is drowned out by the roar of people having a good time.

I told Jack about the Jack rule and reminded him of how it began at a dinner party in the Hamptons on a summer long ago. He smiled; I wasn't sure if he could hear me over the roar of the party. He told me that his back was out and that it was very painful. His doctor had given him three rules, he said: no running, no sit-ting in a soft chair, and no sex. He told me with a grin that he can happily obey two of these rules. I laughed and said that two out of three is really all any doctor expects. "I'm still making the same mistakes," he said. He was alone at the party and has been alone every time I have seen him in the past few years. "I'm still making the same mistakes." The crowd moved us away from each other.

the dog again

This book began with my third wedding, my marriage to a man I thought was the love of my life. That was almost twenty years ago. My daughter was seven, and I was forty-six. The basset hound that ate the cake has been dead for a decade. He has been replaced in my husband's life by another equally naughty basset hound. The son who was born five months after the wedding is now eighteen. I promised to explore the question of whether or not I was acting as an addict or as a woman who had finally found her true love, and I have. The question is explored, but it is still unanswered because in that case, both were true. Addiction is confusing, but it is also hidden and twined around more benevolent feelings. My third husband is a remarkable man, brilliant in many ways, loving and generous too. I think he was the love of my life; I also think he was the perfect expression of my addiction and the ideal reflection of the traumas of my childhood as, I suspect, I was for him.

Nevertheless, although we are still married, we did not stay together. Another addiction, alcoholism, drove us apart. When I stopped drinking, the marriage had to be redefined. I started drinking again. When I stopped a second time, I knew that I could no longer live with someone who was drinking. In order to keep our marriage together, Warren then stopped drinking, but he couldn't stay stopped. We have stayed friends, but at a distance. He lives in California and I live in New York with our son.

Addiction to sex, to romance, to the idea of love distorts many of our lives, and we don't even know it's happening. Whether we are acting out childhood abuse, whether we have a disease that has been passed on in our genetic DNA, whether we are expressing old wounds through a body language that requires a person of the opposite sex, or whether we are helpless pawns in a psychic family lottery, we who are sometimes addicted to other people ruin our lives and theirs. There are many ways to deal with addiction, but before anything gets better, the addiction has to be recognized and acknowledged.

We all know how this book should end. We are all storytellers with an intuitive sense of how narratives should begin with a problem, bounce through adversity and end with resolution. Life doesn't obey the same rules. This story should end when I find the right man and realize addiction-free happiness with my fourth husband. We should be peacefully contemplating old age together, sitting together in the front rows of twelve-step meetings, raising our hands, and having sex that is enjoyable without any of the old sparks or fires of the humiliating past. That's not the story though. Louisa May Alcott, in a similar situation as she finished her masterpiece *Little Women*, cobbled together an elderly professor to marry her Jo

March. Alcott herself never married. She resented having to do that to her story, and that was fiction. This is nonfiction.

Some days the story that began with my meeting Warren does not have a happy ending. Our son has to travel if he wants to see his father; we are not together. Separation is heartbreaking for kids. Other days it seems to have a happy ending. When I was with Warren in the old days, I felt safe and at peace; that was why I had to be with him. But now, falling asleep in my own bed with my son asleep next door and the dog curled in the hollows of his body, I feel safe and at peace.

Perhaps our ideas of happy endings are too restrictive. We think that when someone is sick, the only happy ending is a cure, although sometimes death can be a happy ending. When someone is "in love," the only happy ending is marriage, although even divorce can be a happy ending. When someone is married, the only happy ending is a conventional, long-term monogamous arrangement in which smiling, successful children crowd around the table to eat the Thanksgiving dinner cooked by their mother and carved by their father. There are other kinds of happy endings.

On the morning of September 11, 2001, my eleven-year-old son refused to go to school. He was staying with his father a few blocks from my apartment, and Warren called me to say that our son claimed to be sick although he clearly wasn't sick. In the six years we had been separated, Warren and I had been in and out of each other's apartments often, visiting and caring for our son.

When we first separated, I wanted a divorce, and I took a series of legal steps in that direction, which Warren successfully resisted. So although we have been involved with other people and although Warren lives with a woman he loves in San Francisco, we are still legally married.

On that morning, I walked down the street, and Warren

handed me a cup of coffee as I went into the bedroom determined to get my son out of bed. I didn't have much time to spare; I was meeting a friend for breakfast. It was about seven-thirty in the morning.

My son tossed and turned. He needed to be up to get to school on time. Classes started at nine. I sat down on the edge of the bed and felt his forehead. The room was a mess, with books and papers strewn everywhere and sandwich wrappers pushed off the bed to the floor. My son didn't have a fever, but he complained of many aches and pains and a sore throat. I decreed that he could stay home for a day. Warren agreed. Then I left for breakfast.

Later, after my breakfast had been interrupted by the news, I went back to Warren's apartment to be with my son. Warren made a fresh pot of coffee. With half an eye on the television, I cleaned the apartment, mindlessly putting the books in the bookcase and making piles of papers and picking clothes up off the floor. My son slept as the news of the terrorist attacks unfolded. I tried to call my daughter in New Jersey, but the phones weren't working.

We were safe, but that morning changed everything. The next New Year's Eve, instead of going to see the fireworks in Central Park as we usually do, my children wanted us all to have dinner together. My daughter has mixed feelings about Warren, her stepfather, but on that night she urged me to call him. "I want to be with my family," she said. Warren arrived at my apartment with his basset hound, late as always and armed with his own drink, a huge yellow cup filled with vodka and some ice. We all sat around my dining room table, a table laden with everyone's favorite food: sushi.

The four of us toasted the New Year with apple juice and root beer and vodka as we sat there chatting about nothing. I asked Warren to say grace. "Lord," he said, drawing out the word in a stentorian imitation of a preacher, "we're a bunch of lucky fuckers." My son chortled and reached for a dragon roll. The dogs snored on the floor. Outside, streetlights shimmered on the wintry park across the street and the water of the East River beyond that, where ice floes bumped together as they were swept on the tides first upstream and then downstream as they melted their way to the sea.

bibliography

Buss, David M. *The Evolution of Desire: Strategies of Human Mating.* New York: Basic Books, 1994.

Carnes, Patrick. *A Gentle Path Through the Twelve Steps.* Minneapolis, Minn.: CompCare, 1993.

———. *Out of the Shadows.* Center City, Minn.: Hazelden Information and Education, 2001

———, Robert Murray, and Louis Charpentier. "Bargains with Chaos: Sex Addicts and Interaction Disorder," *Sexual Addiction and Compulsivity, the Journal of Treatment and Prevention* (Philadelphia) 12: 79–120.

Ewald, Roschbeth. "Sexual Addiction." *AllPsych Journal,* May 13, 2003.

Fromm, Erich. *The Art of Loving.* New York: HarperCollins Perennial, 2000.

Hitchcock, Jane Stanton. "A Meditation on Obsession," unpublished ms.

Hoffman, John, and Susan Froemke, eds. *Addiction: Why Can't They Just Stop? New Knowledge. New Treatments. New Hope.* New York: Rodale Press, 2007.

hooks, bell. *All About Love.* New York: HarperCollins Perennial, 2001.

Katz, Dr. Robert. *The Diary of a Sex Addict.* Bloomington, Ind.: First Books, 2003.

Mead, Rebecca. *One Perfect Day.* New York: Penguin, 2007.

Nuland, Sherwin. *The Art of Aging: A Doctor's Prescription for Well-Being.* New York: Random House, 2008.

Peele, Stanton, with Archie Brodsky. *Love and Addiction.* New York: Signet, 1975.

Rogers, Annie P. *The Unsayable: The Hidden Language of Trauma.* New York: Random House, 2006.

Ryan, Michael. *Secret Life: An Autobiography.* New York: Pantheon, 1995.

Scarf, Maggie. *Secrets, Lies, Betrayals: How the Body Holds the Secrets of a Life, and How to Unlock Them.* New York: Ballantine, 2005.

Schaef, Anne Wilson. *Escape from Intimacy.* San Francisco: HarperSanFrancisco, 1989.

Silverman, Sue William. *Love Sick: One Woman's Journey Through Sexual Addiction.* New York: Norton, 2001.

Sternberg, Robert, and Michael Barnes, eds. *The Psychology of Love.* New Haven: Yale University Press, 1988.

Tallis, Dr. Frank. *Love Sick: Love as a Mental Illness.* New York: Thunder's Mouth Press, 2004.

Yalom, Irvin D. *Love's Executioner.* New York: Basic Books, 1989.

More great
Susan Cheever titles

A lively and controversial account of the remarkable intellectual community, including Emerson, Thoreau, Alcott, and Melville, that blossomed in Concord, Massachusetts, during the mid-19th century.

This definitive and ground-breaking biography of Bill Wilson, founder of Alcoholics Anonymous, offers a remarkably human portrait of a man whose life and work both influenced and saved the lives of millions of people

Using the domestic details of her family's life, Cheever reveals the challenges, the joys, and the heartbreaks of being a parent in this engaging and eloquent memoir.

Addressing for the first time the profound effects that alcohol had on her life, Cheever delivers an elegant memoir of clear-eyed candor and unsettling intimacy.

Available wherever books are sold or at www.simonandschuster.com.